How to support and manage
teaching assistants

Acknowledgements

I should like to thank Peter Heath, headteacher of Blakenall Heath Junior School, Walsall, for permission to base the case study of good practice presented in this book on the good practice observed in his school. My thanks also to Michael Fox, headteacher of Busill Jones JMI School, Walsall, and Pauline Williams, teacher at Lodge Farm JMI School, Willenhall.

I am grateful to Vanessa Beecham, teaching assistant at Furze JMI School, Birmingham, for the examples of completed small-group record sheets on pages 35–38; and also to Sheila Scarrott, SENCo, and the teaching assistants at the Oval School, Yardley, Birmingham, for their help in devising the examples for the teaching assistants' handbook in Chapter 4.

I should also like to thank all the many dedicated and hard-working teachers and teaching assistants I have observed, who have been the source and inspiration for so many of the ideas presented in this book.

Finally, I should like to thank Biff and Chip, the two noisy dogs who live over the road, for granting me prolonged periods of silence (no barking, anyway), which allowed me to get on with the serious business of writing this book.

If you would like details of the one-day courses Veronica Birkett provides for schools, please contact her at *veronica.birkett@virgin.net*

For extra copies of this book please call Customer Services on 01945 463441

How to support and manage teaching assistants
LL01718
ISBN 1 85503 385 2
© Veronica Birkett
Cover illustration © Peter Wilks
Inside illustrations © Rebecca Barnes
All rights reserved
First published 2004

Printed in the UK for LDA
Duke Street, Wisbech, Cambs, PE13 2AE UK
3195 Wilson Drive NW, Grand Rapids, MI 49544 USA

Contents

Contents

Introduction

In recent years, the number of teaching assistants has been steadily increasing. For teachers, the presence of teaching assistants must surely reduce the burden and make classroom life easier. Or does it? Making effective use of this resource creates its own particular demands on both schools and teachers. And whilst there is no shortage of training for the teaching assistant, the teacher's need for help in acquiring relevant management skills and adapting work practice has often been overlooked.

The main aim of this book, therefore, is to provide primary schools with clear guidelines for the management of teaching assistants. It offers support for:

- senior management teams, providing a framework for reviewing and deciding on arrangements for the management, support and deployment of teaching assistants;
- teachers, providing insight into the relationship as well as practical ideas for managing teaching assistants in the classroom;
- teaching assistants, providing them with an overview of the job and its wider context as well as tips for working with children and teachers.

Chapter 1
The current state of play

BUT I THOUGHT YOU MADE A RAFFIA MAT YESTERDAY?

YES, BUT THAT ONE WAS ON THE VIKINGS. TODAY I MADE A MAT ABOUT LONG DIVISION

Some children from the beginning to the end of the primary school find such difficulties in learning to do what other children do, that they present problems that worry many teachers … Still others – unfortunately a large group – make little or no progress because they have little capacity. Even to enable them to work to capacity makes great demands on a teacher. How best to help all these children while they remain in ordinary classes with children who are much more able, without giving the class less than a fair share of time to any group, is one of the inescapable problems of class teaching.

Primary Education: Raising Standards, Her Majesty's Stationery Office (1959)

Back in 1959, the responsibility of teaching whole classes, which included those with 'little capacity', was regarded as 'an inescapable problem'. Employing additional adults in order to cope with the 'inescapable problem' was not even a consideration. Rumour has it – there is no corroborating evidence – that the solution favoured by some teachers was to organise the less academic (those with 'little capacity') into groups at the back of the class, where they would be occupied in weaving raffia mats.

Things ain't what they used to be

When my own teaching career began in the 1960s, I did not run a raffia-mat group for my less able pupils, but I am certain that their needs went largely unmet as a result of low expectations, large class size, poor resources and my lack of knowledge about differentiation. These pupils would perform the same tasks as everyone else in the class and my idea of differentiation was differentiation by outcome. In other words, I would accept incomplete, poorly presented work. I would add insult to injury by writing caustic comments such as 'Poor' or the dreaded 'See me'. Thus I was blaming pupils for their failure to complete work adequately, when it was far too difficult anyway. Oh dear. Poor them. Sorry! I can only say that is how things were then. We have all moved on.

The point here is that the task of teaching mixed-ability classes has always been, and still is, a very demanding one. Even though teachers create groups according to ability and differentiate work accordingly, it is still an almost impossible task to meet the needs of all pupils, at all levels, all of the time. In most primary school classrooms, gifted and more able pupils are educated alongside those with learning difficulties. A challenging task. And let us not forget the silent majority: those who are neither more nor less able, and who traditionally have never had any additional classroom support but would benefit if they did.

The task of teaching a class and meeting the diverse needs of all its pupils has become even more challenging over recent years. This has happened partly because of a move by the Department for Education and Skills (DfES) to include

He who in early days was unwise but later found Wisdom, he sheds a light over the world like that of the moon when free from the clouds.

From
The Dhammapada:
Sayings of Buddha,
ed. T.F. Cleary (1995)

pupils with even the most challenging special educational needs (SEN) in mainstream schools, where possible. Further pressure was added with the bid to raise standards through target setting, together with the introduction of the literacy and numeracy strategies. At the same time, schools are required to take account of the needs of more able pupils. How was some of this pressure to be relieved? The answer had to be the introduction of additional adults in the classroom. Previously, the only adult support to be found in schools was a willing mother mixing paint in the corner or hearing the occasional reader. Now, however, we have a growing workforce of teaching assistants (TAs), who are fast becoming competent professionals, able to play a vital role in the function of schools. Their support, used effectively, can help to reduce the ever increasing workload of teachers as well as raising the achievement of all pupils.

So, in the last 40 years we have gone from mainstream classrooms with almost non-existent additional support to a situation where it is expected that teachers will be allocated the support of a TA for at least some, if not all, of the time. The raffia-mat group at the back of the class has long since disappeared (if it ever existed) and all pupils can now expect to be offered meaningful support and the provision of an education appropriate to their level of need.

The teaching assistant – friend or foe?

Whilst the support offered by TAs is undoubtedly welcome, it does create an additional responsibility for the teacher: that of managing another worker. This is not the same thing as managing a class of 30 children, and it is easy to see that if a teacher does not have the necessary skills, then the TA may be seen as an extra pressure, rather than the asset they really are.

Younger, less experienced teachers – through lack of training, awareness and experience – are often not sure what can be expected from their TA. Privately, they may be thinking along the following lines:

> *Oh dear, I don't know what to do with this TA. She makes me feel incompetent. She seems to know much more than I do, but I am supposed to be in charge. I don't like the children always going to her instead of me. Yesterday, when we went to the park, they all wanted to hold her hand and not mine. I felt upset.*

Older teachers, on the other hand, who have followed well-established classroom routines for years, may be resistant to sharing the load. Their thoughts may be rather different:

> *I do not want or need this intruder. After all, things have always worked well before, haven't they? I would rather have spent the money on extra resources. It's just extra work, and I didn't need her in the first place.*

Both positions are completely understandable. To manage a team effectively requires a set of skills not usually covered in the course of initial teacher training. Of course, some may use management skills instinctively or have learned them from experience in other contexts. However, there is no reason to assume that teachers know what to do. And whilst the TAs being introduced into our schools are undergoing all kinds of training, rarely do teachers themselves receive the training necessary to manage them.

Team management should be a standard part of both initial and in-service training, but at the time of writing this is far from being the case. This book aims to provide some help for teachers who have missed out, and some further ideas for those who have been shown the ropes. We shall begin with a closer look at the current situation.

'Team management should be a standard part of both initial and in-service training.'

Standards and qualifications

The current situation for TAs is an interesting and exciting one. The role of the TA has become much more complex, demanding and responsible over recent years. Indeed, the scope of the role has increased to such a degree that there are proposals for appropriately qualified TAs to take over whole classes for short periods of time to allow teachers to carry out their administrative role. The development of the new, higher-level teaching assistant (HLTA) role, for which TAs would need relevant qualifications, would provide a career structure and further opportunity for TAs wishing to develop their careers. The Teacher Training Agency (TTA) has produced standards for HLTAs although final details have not been published. The proposals for HLTA status have come out of the document *Raising Standards and Tackling Workloads: A National Agreement*, which is due to come into force in September 2005. Those with HLTA status will be able to take over classes to relieve teachers and provide them with guaranteed planning, preparation and assessment time, and to reduce the time they need to spend covering for absent colleagues.

Other changes are afoot. Problems had arisen because TA responsibilities had been increasing, but this was not reflected in the pay or in career structure. Some TAs had more responsible roles than others, yet all were receiving similar pay. Some were well qualified for the role – having undertaken accredited courses provided by LEAs, such as City and Guilds certificates in learning support, and specialist TA courses – whilst others remained unqualified. Again, there was no differentiation in the level of pay. The only qualification that attracted a slightly higher rate of pay was the NNEB diploma. However, this also caused resentment, since nursery nurses often found themselves in a similar role to that of unqualified and inexperienced TAs. Finding themselves apparently with the same status as these TAs made the NNEB nurses feel undervalued, and with no incentive to become better qualified many TAs remained in the job without seeking any relevant accreditation. Furthermore, the Local Government National Training Organisation (LGNTO) found that amongst those TAs who did have some kind of qualification, three hundred different types were represented. In view of the growing responsibility of the job, something had to be done to sort out the confusion over the role of TAs and what could be expected from them. To help solve the problem, the LGNTO developed the National Occupational Standards (NOS) for teaching/classroom assistants. NOS were introduced in the summer of 2001. They provide a framework to clarify the different responsibilities and ensure best practice. The LGNTO regard them as an important source of reference for schools that will help them to:

○ audit the skills needed for effective classroom support in their own establishment;

○ identify opportunities for their TAs' career development;

○ develop training programmes;

○ recognise existing skills and those acquired through training and development programmes.

The DfES supported the development of the NOS for TAs. In September 2002, two new National Vocational Qualifications (NVQs) based on the NOS were introduced. I believe this was an important turning point. The NOS indicate that the value of TAs' work has been officially recognised, and will help to create a career structure that is both clear and fair.

An overview of the NOS is provided on pages 10 and 11. Full details can be found on the LGNTO website (see page 64).

Using the standards in school

Schools and teachers can use these NOS descriptions to ensure they have realistic expectations about how they deploy their TAs. This in turn should be reflected in TA job descriptions, with those at Level 2 including different and fewer responsibilities than those at Level 3. Schools could also use the descriptions to ensure that TAs are being deployed as efficiently and effectively as possible.

A training day or series of staff meetings would provide an opportunity for both teachers and TAs to examine specific units and discuss how these are being addressed in their own particular situation. The units to be investigated should be decided by the senior management team (SMT) beforehand to allow teachers and TAs time to think about their current practice.

One school organised a short meeting to examine Units 3.6, 3.8, 3.12 and 3.17. At the meeting, teachers and TAs were allocated to four mixed groups. Each group focused on one unit, asking themselves the following questions:

○ How are our TAs currently employed in this role?

○ Are there any adjustments needed to improve/develop the TA role in this area?

○ If so, how can these be achieved?

The group investigating Unit 3.8, *Contribute to the planning and evaluation of learning activities*, reported back as follows.

How are our TAs currently employed in this role?

Our TAs currently:

- receive copies of the weekly plans on Monday mornings;
- complete record sheets for groups supported in literacy and numeracy sessions;
- complete individual record sheets for pupils with SEN;
- update on-going assessments of sight words and phonics for pupils in Key Stage 1 and for pupils with SEN in Key Stage 2.

Are there any adjustments needed to improve or develop the TA role in this area?

- TAs think it would be helpful to have the opportunity to discuss the plans they are given, especially as some of the suggestions often need clarification.
- TAs would like more time to give verbal feedback to the teacher, because they do not always feel that their comments on the record sheets are taken into consideration.
- Teachers feel the format of the existing record sheets does not allow adequate space for TAs to record some of the information required.

How can these be achieved?

- Some teachers may be able to meet with their TAs to discuss plans while the class are in Monday morning assembly; others will need to arrange a meeting 10 minutes before school begins.
- Teachers should arrange a daily 5-minute meeting to consider feedback from the TA, at a time convenient for both.
- The record sheet could be changed to allow sufficient space for information; one teacher has volunteered to undertake the task.

The value of such meetings is that they raise everyone's awareness of underlying problems. They provide the opportunity for teachers and TAs to share good practice and to discuss issues openly, rather than indulging in chuntering in the staff room — which solves nothing.

The eventual outcome

Two teachers were given permission to meet with their TAs during assembly time on Monday mornings. The remaining six were able to plan their meetings 15 minutes before the start of school. These TAs were to be given time off in lieu. To accommodate feedback, most teachers arranged a daily 5-minute session after school. Two teachers whose TAs also worked as lunchtime supervisors scheduled their 5-minute feedback sessions before the beginning of afternoon school.

National Occupational Standards

Level 2

Unit 2.1 Help with classroom resources and records
Help with organisation of the learning environment
Help with classroom records

Unit 2.2 Help with the care and support of pupils
Help with the care and support of individual pupils
Help with the care and support of groups of pupils

Unit 2.3 Provide support for learning activities
Support the teacher in the planning and evaluation of learning activities
Support the delivery of learning activities

Unit 2.4 Provide effective support for your colleagues
Maintain working relationships with colleagues
Develop your effectiveness in a support role

Unit 2.5 Support literacy and numeracy activities in the classroom
Help pupils with activities which develop literacy skills
Help pupils with activities which develop numeracy skills

Level 3

Unit 3.1 Contribute to the management of pupil behaviour
Promote school policies with regard to pupil behaviour
Support the implementation of strategies to manage pupil behaviour

Unit 3.2 Establish and maintain relationships with individual pupils and groups
Establish and maintain relationships with individual pupils
Establish and maintain relationships with groups of pupils

Unit 3.3 Support pupils during learning activities
Provide support for learning activities
Promote independent learning

Unit 3.4 Review and develop your own professional practice
Review your own professional practice
Develop your own professional practice

Unit 3.5 Assist in preparing and maintaining the learning environment
Help prepare the learning environment
Prepare learning materials for use
Monitor and maintain the learning environment

Unit 3.6 Contribute to maintaining pupil records
Contribute to maintaining pupil records
Contribute to maintaining the record keeping system

Unit 3.7 Observe and report on pupil performance
Observe pupil performance
Report on pupil performance

Unit 3.8 Contribute to the planning and evaluation of learning activities
Contribute to the planning of learning activities
Contribute to the evaluation of learning activities

Unit 3.9 Promote pupils' social and emotional development
Support pupils in developing relationships with others
Contribute to pupils' development of self-reliance and self-esteem
Contribute to pupils' ability to recognise and deal with emotions

Unit 3.10 Support the maintenance of pupil safety and security
Contribute to the maintenance of a safe and secure learning environment
Minimise the risk arising from health emergencies

National Occupational Standards

Unit 3.11 Contribute to the health and well-being of pupils

Support pupils in adjusting to a new setting
Support pupils in maintaining standards of health and hygiene
Respond to signs of health problems

Unit 3.12 Provide support for bilingual/multilingual pupils

Support development of the target language
Help bilingual/multilingual pupils to access the curriculum

Unit 3.13 Support pupils with communication and interaction difficulties

Enable pupils with communication and interaction difficulties to participate in learning activities
Help pupils with communication and interaction difficulties to develop relationships with others

Unit 3.14 Support pupils with cognition and learning difficulties

Support pupils with cognition and learning difficulties during learning activities
Help pupils with cognition and learning difficulties to develop effective learning strategies

Unit 3.15 Support pupils with behavioural, emotional and social development needs

Support the behaviour management of pupils with behavioural, emotional and social development needs
Help pupils with behavioural, emotional and social development needs to develop relationships with others
Help pupils with behavioural, emotional and social development needs to develop self-reliance and self-esteem

Unit 3.16 Provide support for pupils with sensory and/or physical impairment

Enable pupils with sensory and/or physical impairment to participate in learning activities
Implement structured learning programmes for pupils with sensory and/or physical impairment

Unit 3.17 Support the use of ICT in the classroom

Prepare ICT equipment for use in the classroom
Support classroom use of ICT equipment

Unit 3.18 Help pupils to develop their literacy skills

Help pupils to develop their reading skills
Help pupils to develop their writing skills
Help pupils to develop their speaking and listening skills

Unit 3.19 Help pupils to develop their numeracy skills

Help pupils to develop their understanding and use of number
Help pupils to develop their understanding and use of shape, space and measures

Unit 3.20 Help pupils to access the curriculum

Provide literacy support to help pupils access the curriculum
Provide numeracy support to help pupils access the curriculum

Unit 3.21 Support the development and effectiveness of work teams

Contribute to effective team practice
Contribute to the development of the work team

Unit 3.22 Develop and maintain working relationships with other professionals

Work effectively with other professionals
Maintain working relationships with other professionals

Unit 3.23 Liaise effectively with parents

Share information with parents about their children
Share the care of children with their parents

The impact of teaching assistants

Taking this kind of active approach to the management of TAs is no easy task. Initially, time and energy must be diverted from an already busy school schedule to decide on and effect changes to existing practice. How do we know that it will be worth the effort? Is there any evidence that TAs have a significant impact on the education of our children? For the answer to these questions, we can look at research done by Ofsted. They spent a year identifying the ways in which effective schools deployed their TAs and evaluating the impact of their work. Their findings were very positive. This extract from their report highlights characteristics of effective TA work. The lists would make an excellent starting point for any school wanting to evaluate its own practice.

The quality of teaching is improved when the teaching assistant:

- works in close partnership with the teacher who plans well for the teaching assistant's role in the lesson and has good arrangements for getting feedback on pupils' learning and behaviour;
- carries out competently, with the teacher's guidance, a prescribed teaching programme such as ALS;
- interacts with the teacher to make the lesson more lively or to generate more challenging discussion;
- knows enough about the subject to extend pupils' learning, for example by using pupils' errors as starting points;
- has good questioning skills;
- deals with minor behaviour issues and encourages pupils' attention, enabling the teacher to concentrate on teaching whole class;
- has good listening skills;
- is able to manage well the behaviour of pupils with whom she is working;
- enables the teacher to use a wider range of teaching methods;
- enables the teacher to organise the work of groups and individuals so as to match the work more precisely to pupils of different abilities.

In whole class teaching, the teaching assistant helps pupils to learn better by:

- minimising distractions by dealing with individual pupils;
- keeping individual pupils on task by prompting their responses;
- repeating or rephrasing questions asked by the teacher;
- providing additional or alternative explanations for individual pupils;
- providing specialist support, for example for hearing impaired pupils;
- noting pupils' contributions so that the quieter pupils can receive extra attention later;
- supporting less confident pupils or those of lower ability or with SEN to make contributions to the lesson.

During group or independent work, the teaching assistant helps pupils to learn better through:

- providing support for an individual or a group of pupils which enables them to tackle tasks confidently that would otherwise seem too difficult for them;
- giving more individual explanations of the task than is possible for the teacher to do with the whole class;

Instead of condemning people, let's try to understand them. Let's try to figure out why they do what they do. That's a lot more profitable and intriguing than criticism, and it breeds sympathy, tolerance and kindness. 'To know all is to forgive all.'

Dale Carnegie, How to Win Friends and Influence People, *1998*

○ giving the teacher feedback about pupils' learning so that he or she can adjust later lessons;

○ giving pupils immediate and relevant feedback on their work.

From *Teaching Assistants in Primary Schools. An Evaluation of the Quality and Impact of their Work,* Ofsted (2002)

So the evidence, if any were needed, is that TAs have proved their worth and are here to stay. However, the TA can only be as effective as circumstances in the school will allow. The following chapters explore those circumstances from the point of view of SMTs and teachers (and also TAs themselves), examining the ways in which we can create conditions that will enable TAs to make full use of their potential.

Chapter 2
The responsibilities of senior management

Since 1998 primary and secondary schools have experienced an unprecedented amount of reform to raise standards of pupil performance. Over the same period, schools have chosen to employ increasing numbers of teaching assistants, to support the delivery of quality teaching and a modern curriculum. It is encouraging to note that the ample evidence from research and inspection shows that many teaching assistants are helping to raise standards in the classrooms in which they work.

Working with Teaching Assistants: A Good Practice Guide, DfES (2000)

The essence of the successful deployment of TAs lies in understanding the nature of the support they can provide.

From Working with Teaching Assistants, *DfES, 2000*

The huge increase in the number of TAs employed in schools has had major implications for school SMTs. The DfES *Good Practice Guide* says, 'the essence of the successful deployment of TAs lies in understanding the nature of the support they can provide'. It goes on to describe the support as having four strands:

- support for the pupil;
- support for the teacher;
- support for the curriculum;
- support for the school.

We shall look briefly at each of these strands before considering the role of the SMT in the effective deployment of TAs.

The nature of teaching assistant support

Support for the pupil

TAs are employed to support all pupils in the classroom. Most are responsible for offering general classroom support, but some, particularly in secondary schools, are employed to support specific pupils with SEN. Suggestions of ways in which TAs can support SEN pupils can be found in *How to Teach and Support Pupils with Special Educational Needs* (Veronica Birkett, 2003). In the past, there tended to be too much individual input for SEN pupils, who were often isolated from the rest of the class, spending long periods of time closeted with their designated TA. Teachers reported that some pupils would work only when their TA was around, lacking the confidence to do so when the support was not available. This way of working also signalled to the whole class that the pupil was in need of support, which could be embarrassing.

In order to alleviate these problems, teachers began to use the support differently and more creatively. TAs now usually work with their specified pupil within a group where not all the children have SEN, or even as part of the class.

The TA must ensure the pupil is the main focus of their attention, but unobtrusively. Of course, there will still be times when it is appropriate to withdraw a pupil for some individual support.

Many TAs who work as a general classroom support will also be supporting pupils with SEN; they are a part of the whole class and will be included in the less able groups that the TA works with in literacy and numeracy sessions. Not all less able pupils will be identified as having a special need that requires support from a TA. The support for these pupils will be gained from ongoing assessment and from consequent differentiation to ensure the curriculum is meeting their particular need.

Support for the teacher

TA support for the teacher may include routine tasks such as preparing resources or accompanying the teacher to swimming sessions or on school trips. TAs may also be invited to play a role in supporting the teacher with behaviour management, differentiation, assessment, and information and communication technology (ICT). At times, teachers may ask TAs to work with groups of pupils on particular programmes of work. Occasionally, it may be appropriate to employ a TA to act as translator for a child who is not yet a competent English speaker.

Support for the curriculum

TAs in primary schools are most often employed to assist with the delivery of the literacy and numeracy strategies. Some TAs employed specifically to offer support in these areas work on a part-time basis. Those employed on a full-time basis will usually also give support across other areas of the curriculum, such as ICT and PE. They often support practical activities in lessons such as art, design technology and science, which tend to take place in the afternoons. The situation is different in secondary schools, where most TAs are employed to work with pupils with SEN and therefore move around the school supporting the pupils' access to many different areas of the curriculum.

Support for the school

TAs are expected to contribute to the life of the school in general. They may be employed to support pupils by running various extra-curricular activities, for example:

- breakfast clubs, offering breakfast to those that require it;
- after-school clubs, such as dance, drama, music, art and ICT;
- homework clubs;
- school tuck shops;
- the library.

The SMT should take account of all these strands when providing an environment in which teachers and TAs can thrive – for the benefit of all.

Strategic deployment of teaching assistants

The SMT are responsible for ensuring the effective deployment of TAs and need to decide exactly what tasks they should be doing. From their study of 167 primary schools, Barbara Lee and Clare Mawson in *Survey of Classroom Assistants* (1998) identified the ways in which TAs were most commonly deployed:

- 77 per cent supported teachers by working with small groups of pupils within the class in literacy and numeracy;
- 49 per cent supported a number of pupils identified by the teacher, moving round the class to offer help as needed during lessons;
- 43 per cent supported an individual pupil in some or most lessons – these would be pupils with SEN to whom the TA had been allocated;
- 38 per cent provided counselling or support outside the classroom – these would often be pupils identified as having emotional and behavioural difficulties to whom the TA had been specifically allocated;
- 33 per cent provided support for the whole class by moving round the classroom to offer support to any pupil, whenever it was needed;
- 31 per cent provided support to the teachers by preparing or contributing to the production of additional materials, e.g. making games to support pupils in literacy or numeracy and gathering together the utensils and ingredients for a cookery lesson;
- 22 per cent provided support to the teachers by providing information on the content of individual education plans (IEPs) and the needs of individual pupils, raising the teacher's awareness of pupil progress, or lack of it.

Your SMT may find it useful to prepare a similar analysis for the TAs in your school. By raising awareness of the overall deployment of TAs in the school, they will be in a better position to decide where support is required.

'We must employ the right person in the first place and then create an environment where they can flourish.'

Clearly TAs are now fulfilling an important role in our schools, but of course it is the quality and effectiveness of the provision that is important, not simply the tasks they undertake. We must employ the right person in the first place and then create an environment where they can flourish. What exactly are schools looking for? Who is the right person for the job?

Appointing a teaching assistant

There is certainly no shortage of people applying for TA jobs. This is not surprising – it is an interesting and rewarding job with hours and holidays that suit many parents with school-age children. With so many candidates to choose from, how can a school ensure that they select the right person for the job?

The process

Your school has a vacancy for a TA. How do you set about finding a person to fill it? The ideas in this section will help you to work through a process that gives your school the best possible chance of making the right appointment.

Recruiting a teaching assistant – checklist of procedures

- ❍ Draw up a job description.
- ❍ Decide what skills and qualifications would be essential in the person suited to this particular job.
- ❍ Decide what attributes would be desirable.
- ❍ Set dates for the applications deadline and the interviews, having first consulted all those who will need to attend.
- ❍ Place advertisement in the local press and school circular.
- ❍ Decide how many applicants to interview.
- ❍ Sort the application forms, rejecting those that do not meet the basic criteria.
- ❍ Draw up the shortlist and invite the selected candidates to an interview.
- ❍ Draw up a list of possible questions.
- ❍ Ensure there is a suitable room available in which to carry out the interviews.

The job description

All TAs must be provided with a job description. It reflects the agreement between them and the governing body. Drawing up the document before embarking on the interviewing process helps to focus everyone's minds on what the job entails. It may be useful to involve all teachers in discussing the document before the final version is produced. The job description here is an example of what a school might provide for TAs employed to support teachers in a general way in the classroom. The document can be used at the interview to clarify the job details and to help the TA to understand what they would be agreeing to by accepting the position.

Teaching assistant job description

Purpose
- ❍ To work with and support members of the teaching staff in ensuring that pupils receive the highest possible standards of care and education, ensuring that they are safe, secure and successful.

Duties
- ❍ To work within established guidelines to support the teacher in:
  - ❍ ensuring that pupils are safe;
  - ❍ teaching the planned curriculum;
  - ❍ using resources effectively;
  - ❍ creating and maintaining a welcoming and stimulating classroom environment;
  - ❍ encouraging pupils to work and play independently;
  - ❍ evaluating and planning children's work;
  - ❍ maintaining strong home–school links.

- ❍ To be involved in planning and taking the initiative to ensure that the lesson objective is understood before teaching begins.
- ❍ To evaluate designated teaching activities and to feed back to the class teacher.
- ❍ To assist in national and school-based assessments arrangements, e.g. baseline, SATs, ELS, FLS, ALS.
- ❍ To meet regularly with class teachers to plan work, raise concerns and resolve problems.
- ❍ To support teachers and pupils with after-school clubs and other activities as agreed.

Skills and qualifications

Whether the vacancy has been created by the departure of a TA or is a new post, it presents an opportunity for the school to take stock and consider what skills would be desirable in a new member of the staff team. They may include, for example, skills in sport, art, ICT, music, needlework, first aid, sign language or a particular foreign language.

Some kind of qualification would probably be desirable, simply as an indication of the candidate's level of competence and commitment. The ability to achieve a qualification is important since there will probably be an expectation that any new TA will study for an accredited TA qualification offered by the LEA or another recognised body. To appoint someone who already has a recognised TA qualification would clearly be a bonus, but unless the candidate has already worked as a TA in another school, they are unlikely to have one. The type of skills and qualifications you are looking for will depend on the situation in your particular school.

Attributes

As well as deciding on the skills required, schools must also consider what attributes would be desirable in their TA. These may include, for example, knowledge of a particular medical condition (for example, there may be a child in the school with cerebral palsy for whom an assistant with specialist knowledge would be helpful) or familiarity with the locality, which can be very useful. Or it may be that you would like a male TA: if you have a high proportion of pupils living in single-parent families from which the father is absent, you may want to increase the number of positive male role models on the staff.

Case study

Blakewall School needed to replace a TA who had left the job owing to family relocation. In planning for recruitment, the headteacher, John Heath, and the governing body began by making a list of areas in which the school was short of skills. There were several, but they identified three areas of particular need.

Musical skill

They observed that no-one in the school could play the piano, yet there was a reasonably good piano in the school hall. They decided it would be good to have a TA who could play. It would liven up assemblies as well as providing a useful model for the pupils, many of whom had never observed anyone playing a piano 'live'.

ICT skills

The new computer suite offered a wealth of possibilities for enhancing pupils' education and was playing an increasingly important role in the delivery of the curriculum. It would be beneficial to have another member of staff with ICT expertise. At the very least, the new TA should have basic ICT skills.

Gardening skills

The school was very fortunate in possessing a large area of ground where an enthusiastic teacher with a group of pupils had created a lovely garden. There was even a greenhouse that had been donated by the Parent Teacher Association. The teacher had moved on (to pursue a career in horticulture) and none of the staff felt they had sufficient time or interest to maintain the garden. It had become neglected. It would be a bonus if the new TA was someone with enthusiasm for gardening, who could take it on and organise a lunchtime club.

Case study

John Heath knew from experience that although the skills a TA brings to the school are very useful, their personal qualities are equally important. The new TA would be working with senior management, teachers, pupils, fellow TAs, parents, and professionals outside the school. The team decided, therefore, that the ability to communicate well would be particularly important. The position also called for reliability, initiative, enthusiasm, a sense of humour, a positive outlook on life – and experience with children.

They decided that any qualifications – even ones not directly relevant to the role of TA – would demonstrate an ability to succeed. It was also essential that the new TA, if not already qualified, should be willing to undertake an accredited TA course as the school policy was that all TAs should gain suitable qualifications.

John Heath drew up an advertisement based on what the governing body had decided.

Blakewall Primary School
Teaching assistant (full-time)

Required, to start as soon as possible, a permanent, full-time (32.5 hours) teaching assistant, to join our enthusiastic and committed team.

You will be required to support literacy and numeracy sessions in the mornings and to give general classroom support across the curriculum in the afternoons.

Some familiarity with ICT is essential and an interest in gardening and/or the ability to play the piano would be an advantage. A relevant qualification is desirable but not essential, as training can be given.

For further information and an application form or to arrange a visit prior to application, please contact the headteacher.

Food for thought

Hidden agenda

Most TAs currently working in our schools are women. I believe the main reasons for this are the insecurity of the job (many work with temporary contracts), the comparatively low rate of pay and the lack of a career structure. When all the proposed government measures to sort out this situation are in place (see Chapter 1), it is my hope that many more male TAs will be employed. Many of our pupils are brought up in single-parent households where there is little or no contact with a positive male role model. Employing male TAs would be one way to address this problem. Moreover, if female teachers are working with male TAs, pupils will be able to observe healthy and positive male–female relationships. I have seen this work extremely well in some schools. The TA role is not only about raising standards, but also about meeting some of the more profound needs of pupils – an aspect that calls for sensitive awareness and careful consideration. The knowledge that male–female relationships can be positive may be an important piece of learning for some pupils and have far more impact on their future lives than any improvement in SATs results. And of course, at the risk of political incorrectness, one might also observe that male TAs are *more likely* to bring with them certain skills such as football and woodworking, not to mention sheer muscle power for moving heavy things around.

The shortlist

Once the job has been advertised and the deadline for applications has passed, it is usually the headteacher, the deputy headteacher and the chair of the governing body who select the candidates for the shortlist. As they sift the applications, they will keep in mind the desirable skills, qualifications and attributes and reject those applicants who have less to offer.

An advertisement in the local paper and the school circular for a TA for Blakewall received 65 applications. The governors were willing to interview five candidates and at the next governing body personnel sub-committee meeting, John Heath, his deputy and his team of governors sorted the applications. First, they looked for applicants whose qualifications indicated a reasonable level of personal literacy, numeracy and general education.

Next they examined the ages of the applicants and decided that very young applicants may not have had the life experience necessary to undertake a job where integrity based on experience and flexibility are vital qualities. More rejections.

Consideration was then given to the current needs of the school. The group identified the applicants who had one or more of the desirable skills. The letters which accompanied the application forms provided the team with more valuable information. They looked for letters that indicated a genuine interest in the job and some experience of children. Five candidates were selected for interview.

Preparing for the interview

Ensure that the entire interview panel have had the opportunity to study the job description and the references for the shortlisted candidates, and that they are very clear about what the school is looking for.

Your school may have a standard list of questions devised for TA interviews. Below is a list of basic questions that need to be covered. These may need to be adapted and supplemented with other questions, according to the particular post or the needs of the school at that time.

- ○ Why did you apply for this job?
- ○ Tell us more about the qualifications you have.
- ○ Tell us about your previous work experience.
- ○ What qualities, skills and experience can you bring to the job?
- ○ We have given you an opportunity to study the job description. Do you want to ask us any questions about it?
- ○ Are you willing to undertake all the duties mentioned?
- ○ Would you be willing to undertake additional training in your own time to acquire relevant qualifications?
- ○ What experience have you had of working in a team?

John Heath used a set of interview questions similar to those on the list, adding others related to the school's particular situation, to be used for individual candidates as appropriate.

- ○ You have ICT skills. We are looking to employ a TA who would be prepared to support Mrs Brown with the ICT club she runs every Tuesday after school. If we paid you for an extra hour or gave you some time off each week in lieu, could that task be added to your job description?
- ○ We notice you play the piano. Would you be happy to play twice a week in the school assembly?
- ○ We were interested to see that you are a keen gardener. We have an area of ground here in school, commonly referred to as 'a wildlife garden'. It used to be a well-tended plot and we would very much like to restore it. We should like to start a gardening club to provide pupils with an opportunity to learn about and enjoy gardening. If you were appointed to the post, is this something you could consider taking on? We would, of course, give time off each week in lieu.

Interviews are intimidating for all of us because we are facing the risk of rejection, however gently that rejection is phrased. It is therefore important to make the situation as comfortable as you can in order for the candidates to feel relaxed and give a true account of themselves. You should, for example, conduct the interview in an appropriate room: the most suitable candidate could be put off by unpleasant or awkward surroundings. Of course, schools are limited in what they are able to offer in the way of accommodation, but usually it just requires a little thought and a few simple measures (see the checklist on page 22). It's worth making the extra effort, otherwise you may lose the best candidate and end up with someone less suitable for the job, merely because they were the one who coped best at the interview.

On the day of the interview, it is a good idea for the headteacher to go into the waiting area to greet the assembled candidates. They could also tell them the order of the interviews, how long each is likely to last and how they will hear the outcome. (Usually the candidates will go home after their interview and be informed of the result that evening by phone.)

The points on the list might seem fairly obvious and you may wonder why it is included. Unfortunately, I have talked to many TAs who have had bad experiences in their job interviews, and the list addresses some of the problems they encountered. Also, it's all too easy to overlook the obvious in the midst of the demands of a school day.

Case study

Following the interviews, John Heath and the interview panel summarised their observations on the candidates as follows:

① He was well informed about the role of a TA and was keen to help children with learning difficulties. He was also very knowledgeable about ICT. During the interview, however, he found it difficult to maintain eye contact and tended to mumble. Pupils might have difficulty understanding what he says.

② She met all the criteria. In addition she could offer ICT skills, she played the piano and she was enthusiastic about the prospect of running a gardening club. She had a pleasant manner and good communication skills. Here is a likely candidate.

③ Although a mother of pupils at the school who is known and respected by the head, this candidate was disappointing. She seemed too self-assured and the panel sensed it might be difficult for her to work as part of a team or under the direction of a teacher.

④ She met most of the criteria. She had limited ICT skills, but was willing to learn. She could not only play the piano, but also the recorder and flute. However, she seemed to lack enthusiasm for the job and did not display much sense of humour.

⑤ She had enjoyed doing voluntary work in her daughter's school and had been thinking for a few months about applying for a TA job. Meanwhile, she had done an ICT course, being aware that ICT skills are necessary for many jobs. She would welcome the opportunity to work for a TA qualification, as she could see herself developing a career as a TA. She was friendly and relaxed and had excellent communication skills as well as a great sense of humour. And the icing on the cake was that she could play the piano and loved gardening.

The team deliberated long and hard after the interview and it was a close-run contest between candidate number 2 and candidate number 5. Finally they chose number 5, the deciding factor being her previous school experience. They may also have been swayed by her sense of humour. So Mrs Lucy Bright received an affirmative phone call later that evening and was delighted to accept the appointment, subject to the outcome of the statutory police check. The details for candidate number 2 were filed in case any further jobs came up.

Interview preparation checklist

	✔
Arrange for all candidates on arrival to be greeted by the secretary with a smile, words of welcome, directions to the lavatories and an offer of a cup of tea or coffee.	
Designate a comfortable waiting area (not the draughty corridor outside the head's office where there is probably a queue of waiting offenders). The secretary should escort candidates there to await their turn.	
Ensure that the room to be used for the interview is booked well before the day (or you may find the committee of the Mother and Toddler group are already in situ, and they are staying put).	
Place a 'do not disturb' notice on the outside of the door. (An unexpected knock on the door will cause an interruption, which may disturb the candidate and also leave everyone with the uneasy feeling that it may happen again.)	
Put flowers in the interview room. This will make the room look more attractive and it acknowledges the importance of the occasion.	
Provide comfortable chairs in the interview room, preferably arranged in a circle. If the interview panel are placed in a row, the lone candidate opposite may feel as if they are facing a firing squad.	
Ensure that all phones in the room – including mobile phones – are switched off. (Phone rings are as disturbing as knocks at the door.)	

Six reminders for a successful interview

- ❍ Smile!
- ❍ Introduce everyone on the interview panel to the candidate.
- ❍ Draw attention to the job description; ask the candidate if they have any questions about it and clarify points as necessary.
- ❍ Try not to lace questions with educational jargon. There is a lot of it about in schools (too much, in my opinion) and if the candidate has not worked as a TA before, they are unlikely to understand it.
- ❍ At the end of the interview, provide an opportunity for the candidate to ask additional questions.
- ❍ Finally, you could ask the candidate if they would be likely to take the job if it were offered to them. There is nothing more annoying than phoning the successful candidate in the evening with the glad tidings, only to be told they do not wish to accept it. Of course, you cannot guarantee avoiding this situation, but a question at this point may eliminate candidates who have decided against the job on the basis of the interview.

So your school has found a suitable candidate. This is not the end of the story; in fact it is only the beginning. The efficiency of the new TA in the classroom will be influenced by many factors. In the rest of this chapter we shall consider the responsibility of SMTs for the effective deployment of TAs.

Ongoing responsibilities

The way the SMT address the following issues will have a significant impact on how effectively teachers and TAs themselves can fulfil their responsibilities to all pupils.

Deployment of teaching assistants

Many heads would like to provide a full-time TA in every class, but juggling the budget inevitably means compromise. Preference for the placement of TAs will usually be given to:

- ❍ difficult or large classes;
- ❍ classes with large numbers of SEN pupils;
- ❍ inexperienced teachers;
- ❍ classes shared by two teachers (the TA's presence offers some continuity for pupils).

Induction and support for new teaching assistants

Schools have a duty to new TAs to introduce them gradually into their new role. Many schools allow them a week to observe other TAs at work, find out where the resources are kept and make use of the school's library of books relating to the role of the TA (see page 64 for a list of recommendations). An experienced TA may be allocated to act as mentor for as long as they are needed.

Clear line management and role definition

TAs are often confused about who is their line manager. It is important to ensure that they are clear about this. The line manager is usually the class teacher, but if the TA is working specifically with pupils with SEN, the SENCo will be the line manager. In either situation, the class teacher is responsible for overseeing a TA and planning their time when the TA is working in their classroom. If a TA is working in several classes they will have several line managers.

All TAs should be provided with a job description reflecting the agreement made between them and the governing body (see page 17).

Careful consideration must be given to the TA's timetable, especially for those that are full-time. However enthusiastic the TA may be at the outset, if their timetable constitutes a continual diet of unrelenting literacy and numeracy they may quickly become disaffected. Realistic timetabling that allows for some variety is vital.

Some heads, along with the SMT and the governors and in accordance with the recommendations of their LEAs, will have to decide where to place their TAs on the four levels suggested by the DfES.

Career structure and accreditation

It is important that the SMT keep all TAs fully informed about any developments relating to their careers and accreditation or that may affect their job in any other way. It is a good idea to recommend that TAs join an appropriate union, since there are many issues in this field that are as yet unresolved (see Chapter 1).

Training and development

In addition to encouraging TAs to enrol on accredited training courses, you should draw attention to the many other training opportunities and conferences from which the TA may benefit. Schools will have to allocate a budget to this area and should make sure the allocation is fairly distributed amongst the TA team. The head may let TAs know their budget allocation so they can select courses accordingly. Teachers will have to be prepared to be without their TA, and should be warned well in advance about days when their TA will not be present, so the planning may be adjusted accordingly. It is important for the school to take seriously any suggestions the enthused TA may bring back from a course. The head should ensure that the TA has the opportunity to feed back to both teachers and other TAs when appropriate. TAs leave courses full of enthusiasm and new ideas; it is important to set the time aside to listen to these ideas and decide if they could be incorporated into lessons. Teachers can gain from the knowledge TAs glean on their courses, and they in turn should share with their TAs appropriate information from courses they have attended.

Support and training for teachers

Many teachers have been thrown in at the deep end and have had to discover how to manage their TAs through learning on the job and through trial and error. There is nothing wrong with a bit of trial and error, but most teachers would benefit from being offered advice on simple procedures for the classroom as well as help in developing their people management skills more generally.

Time for teaching assistants to participate in other activities

Teachers and TAs will need regular time together to discuss weekly and medium-term planning, the progress of pupils, any behaviour problems, information about the latest training courses either may have attended, and many other things that are part of the TA's job. Teachers, already stretched to the limit, may find this further demand on their time difficult, but it is very important that a regular time is made available.

School activities such as staff meetings, reviews for pupils with SEN or twilight training sessions are often held after school. As TAs are usually paid on an hourly basis for their time in school, they should be financially compensated for time spent after hours, or given time off in lieu.

Case study

For her first week in school, Lucy Bright was given the opportunity to observe various TAs working in different classrooms supporting in literacy and numeracy, and across the curriculum. She also observed two TAs running a dance club at lunchtime and accompanied a teacher taking his class to the swimming pool.

She was shown where all the resources were kept and the small library of books she might find useful. On the last day of her induction week, she spent time in Class 4, where Jan Brown, the class teacher, introduced her to the class.

The headteacher drew Lucy's attention to an LEA one-day training course which would be a useful introduction. He also gave her details of an NVQ2 course for TAs, which would provide her with a recognised qualification.

Lucy Bright was placed with Class 4 in the mornings since it was the policy of the school to have a TA in every classroom each morning to support in literacy and numeracy. In the afternoons, she spent Mondays with Class 4 supporting in music and ICT; Tuesdays with Class 6, taking a group following an intensive literacy 'catch up' programme; Wednesdays supporting a Year-3 group with ICT skills; Thursdays with Class 5 to support a group of more able pupils with a maths programme; and Fridays accompanying Years 3 and 4 to the swimming pool. The decision to move her around in the afternoons was based on the need for her skills in other classes and to share the support across the school. It also acknowledged the importance of other areas of the curriculum as well as offering her more variety. A diet of literacy and numeracy could become very tedious. They wanted to keep her happy.

Jan Brown in Class 4 was Lucy's main line manager, but when she was working in Classes 3, 5 or 6, the teacher in that class would act as line manager.

Lucy agreed to play the piano in assemblies on Wednesdays and Fridays. She also began to help Jan Brown run the ICT club on Tuesdays and received additional pay accordingly. On Fridays she started a gardening club at lunchtime. To compensate for her time, she was given an hour off in lieu, enabling her to leave an hour early on Friday afternoons. When her presence was required at staff meetings after school she was to be compensated for her time.

Lucy Bright and all the teachers she supported were given a copy of her timetable.

Case study

When she had been in the job for several months, Lucy wrote her own, unofficial job description.

- Helping put coats on
- Helping take coats off
- Wiping up unmentionable messes
- Helping to line pupils up quietly outside the class
- Photocopying
- Sharpening pencils
- Supplying spellings
- Offering comfort to pupils (and to the teacher) in times of adversity
- Monitoring the teaching and behaviour of class and individual pupils
- Taking small groups in literacy and numeracy
- Showing pupils how to use the computers
- Sorting out pupils who don't understand how to use the computers
- Planting bulbs
- Chasing stray dogs out of the playground
- Accompanying the teacher to swimming lessons and on school trips
- Removing pupils from class

- Removing staples from boards
- Ensuring pupils enter class in an orderly fashion
- Helping pupils with learning difficulties
- Supporting pupils with special educational needs
- Carrying out literacy and numeracy intervention programmes
- Supporting in other lessons
- Mixing paints and in other ways preparing resources and materials for lessons
- Encouraging reluctant pupils to participate in lessons
- Preparing resources
- Getting out PE equipment
- Putting up displays
- Taking down displays
- Supervising at playtimes
- Selling the school tuck
- Playing the piano at staff parties
- Wiping up tears (sometimes the teachers')
- Making a dozen elf costumes

There appears to be no lack of variety in this job description.

In this chapter, we have looked at the crucial role of the SMT in creating circumstances to enable TAs not only to have a positive impact on the school where they are employed, but also to be provided with opportunities to develop professionally and personally for the benefit of all.

When the SMT have fulfilled their role, it's over to the class teacher …

Chapter 3
The role of the teacher

One looks back with appreciation to the brilliant teachers, but with gratitude to those who touched our human feelings. The curriculum is so much necessary raw material, but warmth is the vital element for the growing plant and for the soul of a child.

Carl Gustav Jung

As Lucy Bright's job description in Chapter 2 shows, a TA can offer support to class teachers in an enormous number and variety of ways: there is no shortage of jobs to be done. Nevertheless, making really good use of the TA in your classroom requires careful consideration and planning. There are six main areas in which a TA can offer valuable support:

- literacy;
- numeracy;
- behaviour management;
- differentiation;
- with the whole class, groups and individuals;
- assessment.

We shall examine each of these areas later in this chapter. But to begin at the beginning, before a new TA sets foot in your classroom it is a good idea to organise an initial ice-breaking meeting to clarify expectations and establish basic ground rules. This will not only make for a much smoother, shorter settling-in period, but may also save the TA from some confusion and embarrassment.

Establishing the ground rules

You won't be able to cover all aspects of the work in one session and it will take time for the new TA to take everything on board. Below are some important points that you'll probably want to touch on in a first meeting.

The role in general

Your TA will need to know exactly what the role entails. You will find it useful to have a copy of the TA job description to hand because the main purpose of this initial meting is to begin to translate this into reality. For example, your plans for the TA may be for them to offer support in literacy and numeracy sessions or to act as a support in other areas of the curriculum. They will need to know what strategies you expect them to use when working with pupils, and they will also need to know what resources will be available for their use.

The TA may be required to carry out specific programmes of work with groups and they may need some training before this can begin. Whatever the exact nature of their job, your new TA should be offered the opportunity to observe other TAs working in similar situations before they are launched into their new role:

> *Your hours have been allocated by the headteacher and governors and are indicated on your timetable. When you are with me, I will mainly need you to offer support to the whole class and groups in our literacy and numeracy sessions. Occasionally I will ask you to work with an individual pupil. The other teachers with whom you are involved will discuss with you how they need you to support them.*

How will your teaching assistant work with pupils?

TAs need to know exactly what their role in class will be. This will vary according to the lesson or part of the lesson. You will need to explain, for example, what you want the TA to do in both the whole-class and the group part of the literacy and numeracy sessions:

> *In Literacy Hour, I will ask you to work with a different group every day. You will know in advance what we will be doing, as I will give you a copy of my plans at our weekly meeting on Monday morning. I will explain more about the plans when we get together and I will also warn you about the difficulties you are likely to encounter with some of the pupils.*

You will also need to make the new recruit aware of general class procedures:

> *If a pupil asks you for a spelling, they should bring you their spelling book. It is the policy in this school to tell the pupil the spelling and for them to write it down on the appropriate page. We believe this system is more likely to help them remember it.*

> *We encourage pupils to drink water regularly throughout the day as there is much evidence to suggest that children do not learn as well when they are dehydrated. Each group has a water jug and each pupil has their own coloured plastic beaker, which they may use to have a drink whenever they wish. Each group has a water monitor who has permission to fill the jug whenever necessary. You and I also have a water jug, of course.*

Where do you want the teaching assistant to be during lessons?

TAs feel much more comfortable when they have an allocated place in the classroom. For group work, this will probably be obvious because TAs will sit with the group of pupils with whom they are working. It is a good idea to allocate your TA a regular place to sit in whole-class lessons. It will probably be a place that offers a good view over all the class:

> *In whole-class sessions such as literacy and numeracy, I will usually want you to sit in a position where you can observe the pupils so you can monitor behaviour, or look out for pupils who appear not to understand. We'll put a chair over there by the notice board for you to sit in during these sessions. Occasionally I may ask you to join a group of pupils on the carpet. Would you be comfortable with that? I don't want you developing back problems on my behalf! When you work with a group of pupils, you*

will join them at their table. When you are working with the whole class, you will spend most of your time walking around the class or sitting next to individuals who may need your help.

What is the role of your teaching assistant in a whole-class teaching situation?

Your TA will need to know what their role is regarding their contribution to whole-class lessons. They may feel uncomfortable and they may not realise that their contribution could be a subtle way of supporting a pupil whom they can see has missed the point, but lacks the confidence to say so. The observant TA can speak on their behalf. Ensure that the TA understands that they have a very valuable role to play in these situations:

Your contributions will be very valuable. It's very good modelling for the class and may encourage them to make their own contributions. It can also be helpful to ask questions on behalf of some of the children, if it's clear to you that although you understand what I am saying, they don't. Your own personal contributions are welcome, too. I often make my own, although I avoid making them too personal. I will tell them news about my dog, but not my divorce!

Another strategy that we could use, if you are comfortable with this, is for you to make occasional deliberate mistakes when answering my questions. I teach the pupils in my classes that 'mistakes are our friends': making mistakes is how we learn, and it is fine to make mistakes. It's all part of the learning process.

Should the teaching assistant mark books?

Teachers usually expect TAs to mark the work of pupils whom they support, but you must show them the marking policy of the school. Make sure they know about practical aspects – for example what colour pen should be used. They also need to know what approach to take – for example what to do with a spelling mistake, how many spelling or grammatical mistakes should be marked in a single piece of work, whether there is a school policy on giving positive comments before suggestions for improvement. Whatever the school approach, it needs to be explained:

When you work with small groups in literacy and numeracy, I would like you to mark the work. At the end of the lesson, I will collect all the books in to check what has been happening. I will also see your remarks on the record sheets you will keep for the groups you are working with. This will help me with my future planning for the children.

Food for thought

Many schools are promoting a more positive approach to marking. It's a far cry from the 'Poor' and 'See me' comments that featured heavily in my early repertoire. It is far more motivating for pupils to find some positive comments, accompanied by suggestions for further improvement – so much more satisfactory than 'Unsatisfactory' (another of my former favourites). They knew it was unsatisfactory, but it was all they could manage. Many must have felt like giving up.

What authority will your teaching assistant have?

Your TA needs to know what rewards they can give: can they, for example, award house points, stickers and other rewards? They also need to know what they are allowed to give permission for:

> If a pupil asks you if they may leave the room to go to the toilet, then it is fine by me to give your permission. However, please remind them of the school rule that they should go to the toilet at playtimes. Pupils with medical problems may have a note which permits them to go at any time. At the moment, however, no pupil in my class has a note.

Your TA will need to know what to do when pupils with whom they are working misbehave. What sanctions are available to them? Can they order a child to stay in at playtime, for example? You will need to be very clear about defining the boundaries. It is helpful to give the TA a copy of the school rules and the behaviour policy:

> If a child misbehaves and it is a minor misdemeanour, such as talking when they should be working, or wandering needlessly about the classroom, then please deal with it yourself. However, if you witness something of a more serious nature, report the matter to me immediately. Do let me know, for example, about instances of bullying or uncooperative behaviour from anyone in your group. I don't want you to have to work with a child whose behaviour you find difficult.

There is more about managing behaviour on page 42.

Introducing the teaching assistant to your class

It is not the practice in all schools, but my feeling is that it is wise for pupils to address TAs in the same terms as they address teachers. In other words, the TA should not be referred to by their first name while you are given the title of Mr, Mrs, Miss or Ms. It is also important to make clear at the outset exactly why the TA is there.

> Good morning, Year 4. Today is a special day for us as we are lucky enough to have Mrs Bright joining us. She will be working with us every morning in literacy and numeracy. I know Mrs Bright will be very happy with us. Let's all wish Mrs Bright 'Good morning and welcome!'

Food for thought

One TA I know had a lovely experience on her first day. When she went to her allocated classroom for the first time, all the children had made 'Welcome, Mrs Jones' cards and they had been pinned to the door. Later that day, they were taken off the door and given to her to take home. It was a great way to welcome her.

By the end of your initial meeting, your new TA should feel reasonably clear about what they will be required to do, as well as when and how. You may find the checklist on page 31 a useful aide-memoire for the meeting.

Checklist of points for a new TA

	✔
The general role of the TA in the classroom	
The three-stage structure of the Literacy Hour, and the TA's role at each stage	
The literacy objectives for the class over the year	
Where the literacy resources are stored and their purpose	
The meaning of terms frequently used in literacy, such as cloze procedure, high frequency words, plenary session	
Class spelling procedures	
The three-stage structure of the Numeracy Hour, and the TA's role at each stage	
The numeracy objectives for the class over the year	
Where the numeracy resources are stored and their purpose	
The meaning of terms frequently used in numeracy, such as mental calculation strategies, negative numbers, ordinal numbers	
Where the TA will sit in whole-class sessions	
The TA's role in the marking of books	
Who are the pupils in class with particular needs, including gifted and talented pupils	
Ways to support bilingual and multilingual pupils	
The TA's involvement with monitoring and evaluating pupil progress	
Ways of differentiating lessons and making appropriate resources	
What assessments are used and why, and the TA's involvement	
The TA's involvement with record keeping and with record storage and security	
The school behaviour policy: the rules, rewards and sanctions	
The TA's role in managing behaviour: what authority they have and which rewards and sanctions they may use	
How to deal with incidents of bullying and racism	
How to contribute to pupils' social and emotional development	
The TA's involvement with parents	
The need for confidentiality	
Health and safety issues	
Emergency procedures	
First aid, and health and hygiene	
How to use the photocopier and other school equipment	
Any other personal equipment the TA needs	
The use of ICT in the classroom	
Safety equipment	
School security systems	

Including your teaching assistant in planning

Your TA will need to be aware of your planning. Ideally, the TA should be included in weekly planning meetings, but often these are held during lunchtimes and you probably complete your plans at home. This may make it difficult to involve your TA directly in planning. Therefore, in order to share your weekly plans, it is helpful to arrange a regular Monday morning meeting — perhaps to take place during assembly. You should provide the TA with all relevant planning information and with record sheets. The planning and record sheets on pages 33 and 34 can be copied for TAs to use for literacy and numeracy. The planning sheet is to be filled in by you before the lesson; the record sheet is for the TA to complete during or immediately after a lesson. See pages 35–38 for examples of completed sheets.

Support for literacy

> The teaching assistant enabled the teacher to use a more effective method of teaching the whole class than she could have managed on her own. The teaching assistant organized the movement of a group of pupils who were holding cards displaying parts of a sentence and punctuation, while the teacher explained what was happening to the meaning of the sentence to the other members of the class.
> Example of good practice, from *Teaching Assistants in Primary Schools. An Evaluation of the Quality and Impact of their Work*, Ofsted (2002)

A new TA may not be familiar with the Literacy Hour and will need to have the structure and implications explained. Before asking a TA to provide support in literacy, you should:

- ensure they understand the three-part lesson structure, as outlined in the National Literacy Strategy Framework, and the type of activities they will be expected to carry out;
- ensure they are aware of the basic Literacy Framework and the criteria that make a pupil literate;
- show them a copy of the literacy objectives for the year groups with which they are working;
- show them the resources that they are likely to need — for example plastic letters, phonics tapes, workbooks and literacy games, demonstrating how to use them if required.

In addition, the TA could be provided with their own set of resources that they are likely to need regularly. This might include scissors, pencils, spare paper, pencil sharpener, dictionaries, word banks and flash cards.

The Literacy Framework contains a lot of complex information and your TA may need further discussions to make sense of it. A new TA should be given the opportunity to observe other TAs supporting literacy, as part of their induction week.

Small-group activity planning sheet

Literacy/Numeracy

Teacher _____

Teaching assistant _____

Lesson day and date _____

Lesson objective
When and for how long?
Activity
Equipment you will need
The outcome

Small-group activity record sheet

Literacy/Numeracy

Teacher _____

Teaching assistant _____

Lesson day and date _____

Name	Comment	Objective achieved?

General comments

Small-group activity planning sheet

Literacy/Numeracy

Teacher __Mrs Brown__

Teaching assistant __Mrs Bright__

Lesson day and date __Monday, 9th June__

Lesson objective

To reinforce cvc work:
To be able to recognise cvc words with medial a, in and out of context, with red group

When and for how long?

After the whole-class shared session for 20 minutes

Activity   Phonics

New phonics blending tape: tape 2 lesson 4. Children to listen to tape and then complete worksheet on page 5. They will need to complete 5 sentences. Ask them for some oral sentences before they write them down. Make sure Thomas is wearing his glasses!

Equipment you will need

Phonics blending tape and workbooks
Cassette player and junction box
Six sets of headphones

Patience and a sense of humour!

The outcome

The group will listen to the tape and complete five sentences on the worksheet. Children who complete the work early should write additional sentences independently in the remaining time.

Small-group activity record sheet

 **Literacy/**Numeracy

Teacher ___Mrs Brown___

Teaching assistant ___Mrs Bright___

Lesson day and date ___Monday, 9th June___

Name	Comment	Objective achieved?
Thomas Smith	Worked well, completed task and wrote 2 extra sentences. Wore glasses.	Yes
Jasminder Singh	Very slow today. Completed task but needed a lot of support and encouragement.	Yes, but more work needed
Suzie Barron	Worked very well. Completed 10 sentences. Ready to move on to work with i, o, e, u.	Yes
Wayne Pugh	Very reluctant to do anything. Tried to distract the others. Only produced 2 sentences.	No, seems very anxious
Jenny Gooch	Completed 5 sentences but very dependent on me for help.	Yes, but needs more practice
Kirsty Williams	Very good indeed. Found the work easy and completed 12 of her own sentences, all correct.	Yes, and needs to work on next stage. Has made great progress.

General comments

The session went well and most of the group tried hard. Wayne and Jenny need some 1-1 work if possible, before the next group session. Am a bit worried about Wayne. Kirsty needs to move on!

Small-group activity planning sheet

Literacy/Numeracy

Teacher ___Mrs Brown___

Teaching assistant ___Mrs Bright___

Lesson day and date ___Monday, 9th June___

Lesson objective

To reinforce recognition of number and amount, understanding the value of each digit.

When and for how long?

For 25 minutes with red group after the mental starter and teaching the lesson objective

Activity

To order numbers to 100 using hundreds, tens and units

Equipment you will need

Numeracy books
Abacus Number Book 2
Pencils
Large wipe board and pens

The outcome

Pupils will be able to order numbers to 100, using hundreds, tens and units

Small-group activity record sheet

Literacy/Numeracy

Teacher _Mrs Brown_

Teaching assistant _Mrs Bright_

Lesson day and date _Monday, 9th June_

Name	Comment	Objective achieved?
Saskia Tumen	Very independent and could follow instructions. No support given. Very good work. Neat and readable writing. Finished topic and given extra.	Yes
Roberto Valanski	Needed lots of support, encouragement and praise. Lacks confidence. Finished task and did a little extra work.	Yes, but needs consolidation
Mustapha Khan	Tended to drift from task. Rushed his work and some was not readable. Tried to distract the others.	Yes, but needs consolidation
Anna Twells	Very quiet and worked well. Some support and plenty of encouragement needed to finish the task.	Yes, but only with support
Jeremy Spooner	Very quiet child, got on with his work but very slow. Only just finished on time.	Yes, just
Emma Knight	Tried very hard. No support given. Finished task and completed all the extra work.	Yes, easily

General comments

Very pleased with how all the group performed. More practice needed with using hundreds. The children tended not to look at the tens numbers, just the hundreds and units. Next time may be ready for thousands.

Supporting in whole-class sessions

The DfES's *Teaching Assistants File* (2000), intended as initial training for TAs, offers some good ideas for teachers on how to make effective use of their support in the whole-class session in the Literacy Hour. They suggest that TAs can assist in the following ways:

- Drawing in reticent pupils who are too timid to put their hands up. Some pupils are daunted by making a contribution to lessons. They may be worried about getting the answer wrong or may simply not like to draw attention to themselves. The TA needs to be aware of these pupils and to support them by giving encouraging eye contact or whispered messages.
  Go on, Manjit, you know the answer to this.

- Or they may need to intervene on the pupil's behalf.
  Mrs Brown, Manjit knows the answer to this.
  Once these pupils realise the world doesn't come to an end after they have responded, they are more likely to make contributions on their own initiative.

- Starting the ball rolling when pupils are slow to begin a discussion. When the room has fallen silent because pupils are reluctant to be the first or are not quite sure what sort of response is required, the TA can step into the breach:
  Mrs Brown, I have some ideas. My favourite season is spring because I like seeing all the trees turning green. And I know what Jane's favourite season is. She was telling me yesterday. Are you going to tell the class, Jane?

- Supporting less able or less confident pupils. It may be appropriate for the TA to sit near these pupils during a whole-class session in order to offer quiet encouragement and to check they have understood.
  Did you understand what Mrs Brown has just said? OK, I'll explain later.

- Joining in and making contributions:
  Oh, Mrs Brown. My favourite Harry Potter book is Harry Potter and the Goblet of Fire. *I have read them all, but I thought this one was best because …*

- Demonstrating for the teacher:
  Year 4, Mrs Brown wants me to write on the board the words you say while she chooses who is going to tell me the word.

- Acting as devil's advocate. When the TA notices that one or more of the class have not understood, they can ask for clarification on their behalf:
  Mrs Brown, I still don't understand what a pronoun is. Could you say a bit more?

- Repeating or rewording explanations or instructions for pupils who have not understood:
  Jamie, Mrs Brown wants you to write the beginning of a story, and then you must ask someone else to provide an ending.

MRS GREEN, I DON'T UNDERSTAND WHAT YOU MEANT BY, 'INTERROGATIVE PRONOUN'.

PHEW...!

○ Acting as an extra pair of eyes. Many teachers find the most effective way of making use of TA support is to use them as an extra pair of eyes during the first half-hour of the Literacy Hour when the pupils are engaged in the whole-class activity. It is essential, however, that teachers explain what the task of the TA is. It must be very disconcerting for pupils to observe the TA writing names down when they have no idea why:

Mrs Bright is helping us again today and she will be watching to see how well you are listening. She is also going to write down the names of children who are not trying very hard and I will speak to those children later. I hope she has no names on her list!

○ Assisting with behaviour management. It may be useful to place the TA next to a pupil who finds it hard to stay on task and is likely to be disruptive. At times the pupil may need to be taken out of the class to carry on working elsewhere. This is another reason why it is important that the TA is involved with the class planning. (See page 42 for more on behaviour management.)

○ Resource management. The TA may be involved with preparing, distributing and collecting pupil resources, and with helping pupils use the resources. They may also help teachers differentiate the resources so they are accessible to all pupils. (See page 45 for more on differentiation.)

The Numeracy Strategy Framework offers teachers guidance on the role of the TA working with groups in the numeracy lesson. I have adapted this to provide similar guidance for teachers to identify ways to utilise TA support in the Literacy Hour, when the TA is providing group support. It could be used as a checklist for the TA.

Checklist for Literacy Hour group work

When supporting groups of pupil within the Literacy Hour, TAs should:

○ ensure the children concentrate, interpret instructions correctly and behave responsibly;

○ remind children of teaching points made earlier in the lesson;

○ question children and encourage their participation (the teacher will need to suggest the questions and prompts that would be appropriate, and identify particular children whom they should focus on);

○ look for and note any common difficulties that children have or mistakes that they make, so that you can address these in the plenary and in future lessons;

○ use, and make available to children, spelling banks, dictionaries, plastic letters or a computer with suitable software, especially when helping young children with difficulties or misunderstandings.

Support for numeracy

Your TA will probably be providing support in numeracy sessions and they need to be supplied with further information in the same way as for literacy. The National Numeracy Strategy Framework contains a section of advice for teachers on how best to use TAs in numeracy sessions:

> The role of the support staff is to ensure that each child plays a full part in every lesson. You should give them copies of this framework (The Numeracy Strategy) and involve them in planning the lessons. You will need to brief them very thoroughly about each lesson and their particular role in it. Make sure they know not only what children are to do, but what they are to learn.

In order to accomplish this, you will need to explain the structure of the numeracy sessions in which your TA's support will be utilised. You should:

- ensure they understand the three-part lesson structure and the kind of activity they will be expected to carry out;
- ensure they are aware of the basic Numeracy Strategy Framework and what makes a pupil numerate;
- show them a copy of the numeracy objectives for the year groups with which they are working;
- show them the resources that are regularly used, demonstrating how to use them if required.

In addition, the TA could be provided with their own set of resources that they are likely to need regularly. These may include scissors, pencils, spare paper, pencil sharpener, number fans, cubes, number lines, 100 squares, plastic number cubes, dice, worksheets and calculators.

The Numeracy Strategy Framework also provides guidance for teachers on the role of the TA in the numeracy lesson. Again, it could be used as a checklist for the TA.

Checklist for Numeracy Hour group work

When supporting groups of pupil within the Numeracy Hour, TAs should:

- ensure the children interpret instructions correctly, concentrate and behave responsibly;
- remind children of teaching points made earlier in the lesson;
- question children and encourage their participation (you will need to suggest the questions and prompts that would be appropriate, and identify any particular children whom they should focus on);
- look for and note any common difficulties that children have or mistakes that they make, so that you can address these in the plenary and in future lessons;
- use, and make available to children, a number line and/or 100 square, visual or practical aids, or a computer with suitable software, especially when helping young children with difficulties or misunderstandings.

The Numeracy Strategy Framework also provides suggestions for working with individual pupils who may need extra support, which, it suggests, should be 'provided discreetly'.

VOLUME? NO PROBLEM —
HERE'S A LITTLE
DEMONSTRATION I
PREPARED EARLIER...

● Prompting shy or reticent pupils. It is advisable to place the TA near to diffident pupils in whole-class sessions. The TA can then observe their responses and quietly intervene when necessary:

Angela, I know you know the answer to this. What is it? Ten, that's correct! Well done. Put your hand up quickly!

● Signing or translating core vocabulary or phrases. Often, the best way of helping pupils to understand core vocabulary (and there is a lot of it) is for your TA to use practical resources to demonstrate the meaning, whenever possible:

Melinda, we are working on capacity this week. Look, let me show you what this means. We can use water and these bottles.

● Helping individual children to use practical resources. Resources such as personal number cards or table-top number lines should always be available to support pupils who may need them. The TA can prompt and help pupils to use them to find the answers:

Jason, use the number line to add 7 and 8. Show me 7 on the number line and now count on 8 places. What is the number you are pointing to? Fifteen. Well done! You found a way of working that out for yourself.

● Operating individual ICT resources as indicated in the children's IEPs. This is particularly relevant for TAs supporting individual pupils with SEN, but all TAs need to know what software is available to promote and support learning with all pupils. You will need to provide some tuition before you ask your TAs to use these resources.

Support for behaviour management

You will need to explain the behaviour policy of the school to your TA, and clarify exactly what you expect of them in delivering it. You must also share information with your TA if there are extenuating home (or other) circumstances that are causing any child distress and affecting behaviour. It is important that teachers and TAs share this knowledge with each other.

Rewards

The rewards to which your TA has access should include the following:

● Verbal rewards:

Well done, Mark! You have finished all your work and it is so neat!

I am very pleased with you today; you did not leave your seat once.

You answered that question very sensibly. Well done!

You have remembered your homework. Good girl!

● Visual rewards. TAs should be able to use stars, stickers or written comments on work:

Brilliant!

● Other rewards. You may ask your TA to suggest a pupil for the 'Star of the Week' award, or to show work in a sharing good work assembly.

Let your TA know that if they witness a pupil achieving something extraordinary, they should inform you so that together you can decide about the level and type of reward – for example a visit to the headteacher for congratulation, a letter or phone call home or extra time on the computer.

Sanctions

The sanctions to which your TA may have access include the following:

○ Verbal sanctions:

I am disappointed with your work. I want you to show that to the teacher. She needs to see you have not been trying hard today.

James, it seems you have forgotten the school rule about talking during our quiet time. Get on with your work, please.

Sultan, I am giving you a choice. If you leave your seat again without permission, then you will move over there to sit by yourself. If you get on with your work and stop wandering around the class disturbing the other children, then you can stay here. What are you going to choose?

○ Visual sanctions. These could include sitting near to the off-task pupil, a stern look, or comments written on books (but making the criticism positive):

I am disappointed with your work. I know you can do better.

I like the ideas in the story, and next time you can give more thought to your spelling.

○ Other sanctions. When more serious misdemeanours occur, then your TA should inform you and together you can make decisions about the sanctions: leaving the class, going to see the headteacher, detention or a letter or phone call home.

If you are concerned about the behaviour of a particular pupil, you may find it helpful to use the behaviour checklist on page 44. Your TA could be asked to tick off the behaviours noted during whole-class literacy and numeracy sessions. They should do this unobtrusively and for a period of a week. The completed checklist provides you with a record of the offending pupil's behaviour pattern. You can use the record to clarify which behaviours the child is most commonly presenting and that information can be used as the basis for setting targets for that pupil. For example, if most of the ticks were by 'Shouts out in class', then the target for the child would be to put their hand up in response to a question or before offering a contribution.

The child should be shown the completed checklist to raise awareness of their negative behaviour. An agreement could then be made between the child and the TA about the support the TA will offer to help the child achieve the target behaviour.

Behaviour checklist

Pupil's name _____

Week beginning _____

Behaviour	Mon	Tue	Wed	Thur	Fri
Shouts out in class					
Verbally abuses another pupil					
Deliberately avoids work					
Late for school or lessons					
Physically abuses another pupil					
Walks about class (inappropriately)					
Changes seat (inappropriately)					
Fidgets/lolls about					
Leaves the class					
Enters room noisily					
Fails to do homework					
Argues with the teacher/TA					
Makes deliberate noise					
Verbally abuses teacher/TA					
Physically abuses teacher/TA					
Mimics teacher/TA					
Refuses to work					
Tells lies					
Throws things around the room					
Refuses to cooperate					
Any other?					

Recorded by _____ Date of completion _____

Support for differentiation

A significant demand on any teacher is the requirement to plan lessons that are accessible to all pupils. In order to do this, the teacher first needs to be aware of the level of the pupils' ability and understanding. The TA can help achieve this by carrying out ongoing assessment.

There are several ways in which your TAs may support you in differentiation. They can do it by:

- direct support;
- task;
- time;
- outcome;
- resources.

Direct support

TAs may offer direct support to pupils by sitting with either a small group or an individual to offer encouragement or direction, to check spellings, to help pupils with their own planning and to answer questions. The support should not be confined to the less able pupils; high achievers would also benefit. Nor must we forget the middle of the roaders who may be overlooked but whose progress, like everyone else's, would accelerate given extra support and encouragement.

'Your TA will not be giving effective support if they are employed merely as a worksheet assistant.'

Your TA will not be giving effective support if they are employed merely as a worksheet support assistant. Suppose the class is being taught about the Romans. If all the class are given identical worksheets to complete and your TA is placed with the less able group, simply to assist with the completion of the worksheet, then very little will be achieved. The less able pupils will not necessarily be able to read or understand what they have written, despite the fact that their completed worksheets look identical to those produced by the rest of the class. What have they learned? Very little. Except, possibly, that they are unable to work without the presence of adult support. How much more effective it would be to ask your TA to talk to the group about what they have learned, to develop their learning through discussion and then consolidate that learning by making a model or producing a play for the rest of the class. For evidence of what has been achieved (since no worksheet will have been produced) the use of a digital camera and a display of photos in pupils' work folders should suffice.

Task

When pupils are working in groups, the same objective may be achieved through different tasks. For example, if pupils are asked to write a story in literacy, it may be more appropriate for the less able group to be given a set of pictures to sequence into the correct order. After that they could write sentences underneath, supported by the TA. A more able group could be put with a TA for a brainstorming session to stimulate ideas. They could then work individually to produce a story reflecting their level of writing skill. The TA would offer support by helping with grammar and spelling as well as sentence and

To be a teacher in the right sense is to be a learner. Instruction begins when you, the teacher, learn from the learner, put yourself in his place so that you may understand what he understands and in the way he understands it.

Søren Kierkegaard

paragraph construction. Another possibility is for the TA to work with a mixed group to share ideas and work cooperatively on the production of the story. With a different approach, the same task does for all.

Time

Some pupils will require more time to finish whole-class activities than others. It may be appropriate for the TA to work with pupils who need extra time. This time should not impinge on their access to the rest of the curriculum, or take them away from a favourite lesson. It is very frustrating for pupils not to have the opportunity to complete work and it also means they move on to the next lesson without having fully consolidated the learning from the previous one.

Outcome

Sometimes differentiation might take the form of different expectations, set according to pupils' capabilities. For example, for one child it might be appropriate to complete ten problems in maths, and for another it would be a great achievement to complete five. If you differentiate by outcome, the TA must be aware of the appropriate outcomes for the pupils they are working with.

Resources

The TA could collect the relevant resources before the lesson. The resources pupils need may be different according to their ability and preferred learning style. Plastic letters will be needed by some pupils to assist with spellings; plastic numbers will be needed by some working on number bonds. Some pupils will require simpler worksheets than others. Less able pupils may need cloze procedure activities, while others may be able to complete independent sentences in their workbooks. Some pupils will be able to use dictionaries to support them with spellings while others may need an individual word bank.

Word banks may be useful for pupils of all abilities as a means of introducing new vocabulary. Each child may be provided with a word bank when new topics are introduced – in science, history, RE or geography, for example. The TA could prepare the word banks in advance, with the key words supplied by the teacher. Sometimes, it may be more appropriate to use word banks with particular groups: for the more able to introduce more complex words to extend their vocabulary, and for the less able to include words appropriate to their level of need.

Lucy Bright was supporting a less able group in a Year-4 class who were doing a history topic on the Tudors. Each child in the group was given a topic word bank and whenever a new word was introduced, Lucy made sure they had entered it correctly.

Word Bank

Name   Lisa Derry

Subject   The Tudors   Class   4

Aa Anne Boleyn	Bb beheaded	Cc Catherine of Aragon	Dd divorced	Ee Elizabeth
Ff	Gg	Hh Henry	Ii	Jj Jane Seymour
Kk	Ll	Mm	Nn	Oo
Pp	Qq quail	Rr	Ss Spain Shakespeare	Tt
Uu	Vv	Ww wattle war	Xx	Yy
Zz				

Support for the whole class, groups and individuals

There are many ways in which your TA may support you in class. You may like to use the following suggestions as a checklist for your TA, ticking off the ones which are relevant to your situation. The list could act as an official agreement about the exact nature of the TA's role in your class, which both of you sign.

Teaching assistant's checklist: supporting the teacher

The teaching assistant's role includes the following tasks:

Helping the pupils catch up with work they have missed	
Reading stories to pupils, or hearing them read, on an individual or small-group basis	
Supervising practical work	
Adapting materials to support pupils in different areas of the curriculum	
Sharing books with pupils for enjoyment or as an aid to comprehension	
Helping pupils with spellings	
Keeping the pupil and others on task	
Reporting back to the teacher, especially problems or successes	
Accompanying pupils who are accommodated in special units to classes in mainstream schools	
Working with pupils on computers	
Observing a pupil's way of performing a task, and demonstrating an alternative way to enable the child to work independently	
Helping younger pupils to change for PE, games or swimming (or older pupils who have physical disabilities)	
Reading textbook sections or questions to the pupil	
Encouraging the use of a tape recorder or dictation machine for recording information – you may need to transcribe what the pupil dictates	
Preparing equipment for cooking, science, art, design and technology and so on	
Contributing to planning and review meetings concerning the pupil	
Accompanying pupils on school trips/visits alongside teachers	

Teaching assistant's checklist: supporting the teacher

Ensuring pupils interpret instructions correctly	
Reminding pupils of relevant teaching points	
Encouraging pupil participation	
Clarifying points and repeating instructions given by the teacher	
Making notes on behalf of the pupil as the teacher is speaking, to use later	
Acting as a scribe for a group or individual pupil	
Joining in whole-class sessions and making contributions	
Explaining words the pupil does not understand, encouraging and teaching the use of dictionaries and spelling banks	
Playing games with a pupil or small group	
Checking the work pupils produce and helping them to correct their own spelling/grammatical errors	
Assessing pupils	

Checklist completed and agreed on (date) _____

Signature of teacher_____

Signature of teaching assistant _____

Support for assessment

Teachers will undoubtedly benefit from their TA's involvement with the ongoing assessment procedures in the class. Your TA could, for example, check sight and spelling vocabulary or mathematical skills – for all pupils or for selected individuals. They can provide valuable assistance with SATs at the end of Key Stages 1 and 2.

TAs can also carry out other types of assessment.

Case study

Jan Brown had an interest in learning styles and wanted to assess all her pupils in this area to help with differentiation. She decided to use Alistair Smith's learning styles test from *Accelerated Learning in the Classroom*, and asked Lucy Bright to carry out the assessment on every pupil. Jo Brown then considered how to involve Lucy in the preparation of resources to match pupils' learning styles.

The teacher was aware of the effect that low self-esteem may have on pupil performance. Although she believed she was aware of 'at risk' pupils, she decided to ask Lucy Bright to carry out the self-esteem test on the whole class, using the assessment from *Insight Primary: Assessing and Developing Self Esteem* by Elizabeth Morris. She planned to introduce a programme aimed at raising the self-esteem of targeted pupils, based on the ideas presented in the book. Lucy Bright would play an important part in the implementation.

We have looked at ways in which you could use your TA's precious time. The effect of the support they give will be either enhanced or impaired by the quality of the relationship between you and the TA. Of course, the issue isn't quite so simple as that – human beings being what they are. Indeed, this aspect might be your main challenge – and it cannot be met by ticking a checklist. You may be lucky enough to have a relationship that's been easy and positive right from the start. But it doesn't always happen like that. So what can you do to create a positive working relationship?

A good working relationship

I think the sign of a good teacher–teaching assistant relationship is when a casual observer has difficulty in identifying which of them is the teacher and which is the assistant. I would describe a good working relationship as two parts of a jigsaw. She [the TA] not only does all the formal things we discuss in the planning, but she brings humour and energy into my room. We all benefit from her presence. It's not only because of work she does; simply having another opinion is useful. It's like having a second pair of eyes. I really miss her when she's not there.

Pauline Williams, Lodge Farm JMI School, Willenhall

The following comments were all made by TAs. They serve to highlight some common likes and dislikes and point towards what is required to ensure the development of a good working relationship.

I hate it when the teacher does not introduce me to the class and the children just look at me sitting there and don't know who I am.

When the teacher introduced me to the class he said, 'This is Jason's mum,' and asked them to call me by my first name. Jason was embarrassed and I felt the children did not have much respect for me. One child said, when I asked another to get on with his work, 'Oh, it's only Jason's mum.'

I like it when the teacher introduces me to the class in a respectful way. Mrs Jones said, 'I want to introduce Miss Day. We are very lucky to have her. She is going to help us with our work. We would all like to welcome her here.'

Be respectful.

One of the teachers I had was very patronising and treated me like one of the children. I hated going into her class. I can't remember ever receiving a thank you for anything I did. I only carried on because of the children.

I was never invited to any planning meetings, or ever shown copies of plans in advance. She would usually tell me what she wanted me to do a minute before the lesson began, and I had no time to think about it. Sometimes she didn't give me any information about what exactly she wanted me to do, and sometimes I sat there feeling I was wasting my time being there.

She is always clear about what she wants me to do, and then never forgets to thank me afterwards.

Be clear and be appreciative.

He always asked me to work with the low ability group. It would have been better for me and them to have had a change, but when I said this to the teacher, it was clear he was not interested in my opinion and did nothing about it.

Sometimes I feel the teacher doesn't know what to do with me and I just sit there wasting my time. I have asked her if there is anything useful I could be doing, but she just says, 'Do what you want.'

We go through the plans every week and he always asks my opinion. He seems interested in what I have to say about the pupils, and often takes on board some of my ideas in his lesson plans. I feel valued.

Be interested.

Last week the teacher asked me to read a story to the pupils. Billy asked me a question and when I had answered him, the teacher cut across me and said, 'That's not right, is it, children? Who can give the correct answer?' I felt terrible.

The teacher I had last year was not understanding when I had to take some time off to attend hospital appointments. I had tried to arrange them out of my school time, but the hospital could not change them. She never asked me how I got on when I came back. It made me feel awful.

She treats me like a human being and always asks me how I am coping with my groups, if all the pupils behave well and so on. When I was in hospital last year she came to see me and all the children had done get well cards. It was lovely.

Be compassionate.

Teachers asking me to do jobs for them when I am supposed to be with another teacher is really frustrating. I do not like to say no, but then I get black looks from the teacher when I turn up late.

I do not get enough help with badly behaved children in my group. I think the teacher just likes to get rid of them onto me. I do not have enough experience to deal with uncooperative children.

The teacher always used to say to me that if any of the pupils misbehaved, then I must not feel I have failed but send them to him immediately. Also, if there were any I felt I could not manage in the group, then he would withdraw them. I think this gave me confidence, and I never asked him to withdraw anyone.

Be fair.

I don't feel I am given enough praise for what I do, so I am not sure if she thinks I am doing a good job or not.

Sometimes the teacher ignores pupils who cheek me, and I feel embarrassed and don't know how to handle it. I asked her if she could give me some advice, but she said to me that if she had the answer to how to deal with kids who misbehave, then she would be a rich woman. It didn't help me at all, and I never asked her for advice again.

He helped me when he heard a pupil cheeking me, not in a way I found embarrassing and patronising but in a supportive way, if you know what I mean.

Be supportive.

I once had a teacher who asked me to fill in record sheets all the time about what the pupils had done, but she never read them. I must admit I stopped writing them in the end, and she never even noticed.

Last week I went to a brilliant course for teaching assistants on the Literacy Hour. The next day I couldn't wait to get to school to tell the teacher about all the great ideas I had learned, and would like to try out with my group. She was not in the least interested and said she was sorry, but there was already too much to do, without taking on any more ideas. I felt the school had wasted precious money sending me on the course. What was the point?

She always reads the reports I write, and always tells me what has happened in the planning meeting. She was really keen to try out some ideas I picked up on this course I had been to, and then said she had seen a course for both teachers and TAs to attend and would I like to go with her? Of course I would.

Take the TA's comments seriously.

Teachers sometimes use jargon I don't understand. It makes me feel stupid.

All of us feel like second-class citizens — we are not invited to staff meetings or planning meetings, and we have our own room to sit in. We don't mix with the teachers at all.

The staff meetings are after school and I do not have to go, but the teacher always tells me what has happened.

Be considerate.

Last Christmas the teachers all went out together for a meal and suggested we all went out together as a group as well. We wanted to be with the teachers, and in the end we did not go out ourselves. I felt disappointed not to be included.

Sometimes the teachers meet to go ten pin bowling together. They have to sign their names on the list on the notice board. No-one ever asks any of us if we would like to go, so last week we all added our names! No-one said anything, but they all went without us, nevertheless.

I enjoy the company of the staff. They treat me like one of them and always invite me to any staff dos they have.

Be hospitable.

As these comments reveal, a good relationship comes largely from an awareness of what it's like to be in the TA's shoes. And a positive relationship is crucial. Without it you will not get any commitment from your TA. You will not have the positive feeling in your class that you get when two people are working well together. You will not get effective support for your pupils or yourself. But with it, you may find your job as a teacher takes on a new lease of life: there's less stress, more time for yourself and a happy and successful class.

Chapter 4
The teaching assistants' handbook

As we have seen, the role of the TA is very varied. It will vary according to the level of the individual job, whether the job is part-time or full-time and whether the TA is employed to assist an individual pupil or to assist more generally. It will also be affected by the skills and qualifications the individual TA has to offer. Keeping everyone in a school abreast of arrangements for their TAs can be quite a challenge. One way of doing this is to bring together all the information relating to TAs in a handbook.

The information found in the handbook usually already exists in schools in some form but, being scattered around, its use is limited. Ideally, the handbook should be compiled as a result of teachers and TAs meeting together to decide what information should be included. The meeting would also provide an opportunity for teachers and TAs to share existing good practice, which would be recorded in the handbook. Following the meeting, it is best if one TA is given responsibility for doing the compilation.

The handbook will need to be updated regularly to reflect the changing situation in your school. The TA responsible for the handbook could be allowed some time at the beginning of each term to review the contents and update the information. An overall evaluation of the contents might be done by all the teachers and TAs at an annual meeting.

Those who will benefit from the information contained in the handbook include:

- governors;
- headteachers and senior management:
  - to gain an instant overview of existing arrangements;
- class teachers;
- supply teachers, newly qualified teachers and teachers returning after some time out:
  - to raise awareness of the many ways in which TAs may be deployed;
  - to make available a better understanding of the role of the TA in order to promote conditions that ensure effective management;
- TAs:
  - as part of their initial induction;
  - to clarify what is expected of them by each particular teacher, in order to create an immediate informal contract;
  - to raise their own understanding of the possibilities of their role as a means of increasing their own personal effectiveness;

Education is not the filling of a pail, but the lighting of a fire.

William Butler Yeats

○ Ofsted inspectors:

  ○ to provide accessible information on the ways in which TAs are currently deployed within the school;

  ○ to provide a greater understanding of what to expect from TAs during inspection periods.

Ultimately, since the contents of the handbook may contribute to the efficiency of the school and the effectiveness of the teaching, those who will benefit most are the pupils themselves and their parents.

The rest of this chapter provides a framework for a handbook. For each section there is a description of the information contained in it, followed by a sample page and then a case study example of a situation in which it might be useful. The exact contents of your handbook will, of course, depend on your particular school; you may need to remove, add or adapt sections according to circumstances.

The handbook sections are as follows:

○ Introduction

○ Who we are and what we do

○ Timetables: where to find us

○ Our skills

○ How we can help: in the classroom

○ How we can help: managing behaviour

○ How we can help: supporting pupils with special educational needs

○ How we can help: supporting supply teachers

○ Additional ways in which we can support the school

AND YOUR TAS CAN FOUND ...?

... ALL IN HERE!

OFSTED

Food for thought

While writing this book, I have been reflecting on my experience of school, first as a pupil and then as a teacher. I believe one of the most fundamental changes that has occurred has been the employment of well-trained additional adults in the classroom. I am certain that teachers starting off in this decade who are given the support of a TA have a marked advantage over those of us who began in the 1960s. My belief is that two heads are better than one, and the combination of an effective teacher with a well-managed, well-informed, trained and motivated TA must make a real difference to the pupils who are in their classes.

Introduction

This gives basic information about the school and explains the purpose of the handbook.

The Firs School

Teaching assistants' handbook

The information in this handbook has been compiled by the teaching assistants at this school, and is updated every term. It is hoped the information will be useful to:

- senior management;
- class teachers;
- teaching assistants;
- newly appointed and newly qualified teachers;
- supply teachers or those working on temporary short-term contracts.

Who we are and what we do

Adrian Williams

I work as a general support assistant in Year 6. I am full-time and have a permanent contract. In the mornings I support literacy and numeracy, and in the afternoons I provide support across the rest of the curriculum.

Jeni Cheng

I work part-time as a general support assistant in the mornings with Year 5, helping with literacy and numeracy. I have a temporary contract.

Sally Potter

I am employed by the LEA to support a pupil with special educational needs (who has hearing impairment) in Reception. I work for 5 hours a week and my contract is temporary.

Who we are and what we do

This section identifies who the TAs are, where they are employed in the school and the different roles they undertake.

Case study

I'm worried about Hanna in my class – I am sure she has hearing difficulties. I have spoken to the SENCo and the school is waiting for further assessments and advice from the LEA. But what should we do in the meantime? I saw from the TA handbook that Sally Potter, working in Reception, has some experience working with a pupil with hearing impairment. I will approach Sally to see if she could give me and my teaching assistant some ideas on how we can best support Hannah until the LEA are able to provide some support.

Steve Jones, Year-3 teacher

Timetables: where to find us

All TA timetables are set out here. This is useful, for example, if a teacher needs immediate information or support from their TA, who is currently supporting in another classroom: they can see immediately where to find them. The information can also be used by senior management to ensure fair and purposeful distribution of TAs amongst the teachers. It can help them to ensure that all the skills TAs bring to the school are fully utilised. School secretaries will find it helpful if they need to find a TA to take an urgent phone call.

Timetables: where to find us

Adrian Williams: Year 6 (full-time)

Monday	Tuesday	Wednesday	Thursday	Friday
Year 6 Literacy Numeracy	Year 6 Literacy Numeracy	Year 6 Literacy Numeracy	Year 6 Literacy Numeracy	Year 6 Literacy Numeracy
Science Swimming (School pool)	Music (Music Room) Geography	Art Extended writing	PE (Main Hall) ICT skills	Games (outside if fine, Small Hall if not) RE
			Gardening Club (meet in the Small Hall) (3.15–4.00)	

Jeni Cheng: Year 5 (mornings only)

Monday	Tuesday	Wednesday	Thursday	Friday
Year 5 Literacy Numeracy	Year 5 Literacy Numeracy	Year 5 Literacy Numeracy	Year 5 Literacy Numeracy	Year 5 Literacy Numeracy

Sally Potter: Jamie Lee in Reception (5 hours weekly)

Monday	Tuesday	Wednesday	Thursday	Friday
Precision teaching 1:1 (10 minutes)	Precision teaching 1:1 (10 minutes)	Precision teaching 1:1 (10 minutes)	Precision teaching 1:1 (10 minutes)	
Daily speech activities (monitored by the speech therapist) (5 minutes)	Daily speech activities (monitored by the speech therapist) (5 minutes)	Daily speech activities (monitored by the speech therapist) (5 minutes)	Daily speech activities (monitored by the speech therapist) (5 minutes)	
Literacy (group) (one hour)	Literacy (working 1:1) (one hour)	Literacy (group) (one hour)	Literacy (working 1:1) (one hour)	

Case study

Sophie, will you go to Year 6 and say to Mr Williams that Harjit has cut his hand with a craft knife and we need him to come and do some first aid? You will find him in the Music Room.

Sandra Charles, Year-4 teacher

Our skills

The handbook should be focused on skills rather than qualifications. TAs can bring many skills, talents and interests into school, and this is a good way to ensure that other people know about them. For example, you might have an ex-county gymnast. What an asset that would be: for lunchtime or after-school gym clubs, coaching pupils with potential, producing gymnastic displays at school and assisting teachers with ideas for PE. You probably have a mine of potential in your TAs. Don't waste it.

Our skills

Adrian Williams
- I worked in an office as a secretary for three years.
- I have a first-aid qualification.
- My main hobby is gardening. I am a really keen gardener and am doing a course in garden design.

Jeni Cheng
- I can play the piano (Grade 7).
- I am interested in all forms of dance. I have a teaching qualification in jazz dance and have done some teaching at a local dancing school.

Sally Potter
- I enjoy sport, especially badminton. (I used to play for my school.)
- I am a keen swimmer and have a life-saving qualification.
- I have a particular interest in working with pupils who have speech and language difficulties.

Case study

Jeni, I noticed it says in the TA handbook that you're a qualified dance teacher. I know there are lots of children in my class who would love the opportunity to do some dance. We wondered if you would be prepared to run a weekly dance club in school lunchtimes for Year-6 pupils. The head has agreed and says that you will be paid for your time.

Tony Fox, Year-6 teacher

How we can help: in the classroom

This list identifies all the ways in which TAs can support teachers in classrooms. The list will be of particular benefit to:

- ◐ class teachers – raising their awareness of options and bringing clarity to what may be expected from TAs;
- ◐ supply teachers – providing a quick résumé of possibilities for them;
- ◐ NQTs experiencing their first taste of real school life, who may not be familiar with the role of managing the TA;
- ◐ teachers returning to the job after time out, who are experiencing their first taste of TA support;
- ◐ TAs – explaining who everyone is, what the possibilities of their role are, and what teachers expect from them.

How we can help: in the classroom

Managing resources
We can help with:
- making resources;
- distributing and collecting resources;
- adapting resources to meet the needs of particular pupils;
- helping pupils to select and make efficient use of resources;
- providing suggestions for teachers about the type of resources observed to be most/least beneficial to pupils.

Delivering specific programmes of work
- Springboard Maths to Year-5 pupils
- Further literacy support to Year-5 pupils
- Additional literacy support to Year-3/4 pupils
- Early Literacy Support to Year-1 pupils

Assisting with the whole class
We can:
- supply spellings;
- make contributions and encourage pupils to do the same;
- repeat instructions;
- encourage pupils to participate in discussions;
- demonstrate for the teacher;
- sit with groups or individual children;
- monitor the behaviour of children by acting as a second pair of eyes;
- observe which pupils appear to be struggling with the work.

Assisting with group work
We can:
- hear pupils read;
- guide and support pupils with writing and spelling;
- initiate and support group discussion;
- support individuals within the group who may require extra support;
- observe, assess and keep records for feedback to the teacher.

Assisting with individuals
We can:
- check understanding;
- repeat instructions;
- provide spellings;
- hear individual readers;
- answer and ask questions;
- accompany children to the library to select books;
- encourage reticent pupils to go to the teacher and ask questions;
- offer praise;
- mark work;
- keep pupils on task;
- complete assessments of work, e.g. sight words, spellings, tables.

Case study

Sam Henman, a newly qualified teacher in charge of Year 5, is shown the list by Jeni, the TA who is there to support him in literacy. He looks at the list of ways in which the TA can support him, and also at the list of how she can give support with behaviour. He identifies from the list all the ways in which he would want her to offer support. Both parties now have a clear idea of their role.

Jeni, I would like you to observe all the pupils while they are in the whole-class session and write down the names of pupils who are not paying attention. Yesterday, there was a lot of talking every time my back was turned, and I need your help to identify the culprits and tell them this list will be left for their teacher. Also I would like you to be seated close to Sophie. I am taking heed of your warning that she attempts to be disruptive every time a supply teacher has the class. Please take her to the head if she continues to be disruptive. Is that OK?

How we can help: managing behaviour

This identifies ways in which TAs may assist with the management of behaviour. This is sometimes a grey area for them and they need to know what their position is. Are they permitted to apply rewards and sanctions? The list suggests possibilities; teachers need to identify the ones they feel would be appropriate for their own particular TA to apply.

How we can help: managing behaviour

The ways in which we can help teachers manage behaviour include:
- sitting near pupils who find it difficult to stay on task;
- removing pupils from class at the teacher's request to offer them an opportunity to calm down;
- walking around the classroom to act as an extra pair of eyes;
- completing behaviour checklists to identify particular behaviour patterns of pupils;
- acting as a behaviour monitor by writing down the names of pupils who misbehave;
- observing potential trouble and stepping in to act as mediator;
- giving non-verbal signs to pupils such as a stern look, frown or hand movement (verbal comments may interrupt the lesson);
- talking to pupils about their behaviour to explain why it is unacceptable;
- encouraging pupils to stay on task by offering positive comments in appropriate situations.

We can offer positive comments when they have:
- come into the class quietly;
- brought back homework;
- completed a piece of work neatly, quickly or accurately;
- been kind to another child (or to us);
- listened well;
- followed instructions;
- been polite to a visitor in the school;
- remembered books or sports gear;
- contributed to the lesson;
- read well;
- brought something in from home for the lesson;
- succeeded with an activity out of school;
- worn their school uniform;
- arrived on time (if this is a problem).

Case study

Elaine Andrews, in Reception, is having problems with one particular boy in her class. He already receives support from Sally, her TA. She needs some help. She reads through the section from the handbook regarding managing behaviour and thinks she has found the answer:

Sally, I would like you to complete the behaviour checklist for Tony every day this week, please. I am very concerned about his behaviour at the moment and we need to set some targets. If you do this, by the end of the week we should have a clear idea of what behaviours are causing the problems. Also, when we do the group work in literacy, I would like you to sit near to him. He is continually trying to disrupt the others.

How we can help: supporting pupils with special educational needs

This section demonstrates many ways in which TAs may support pupils identified as having SEN, although this will of course vary according to the nature of the need.

How we can help: supporting pupils with special educational needs

We can:
- work on targets on IEPs;
- work on particular programmes of work;
- oversee exercise regimes recommended by physiotherapists or occupational therapists;
- adapt resources to meet the needs of individual children;
- make resources;
- oversee and maintain equipment used by pupils with SEN, e.g. hearing aids and wheelchairs;
- inform teachers of problems observed during sessions, e.g. noticing if a pupil is often tired or hungry or if any suspicious marks appear on the child's body (this applies also to any other pupil we may support in class);
- keep records of pupil progress to help teachers plan future lessons;
- encourage pupils to work independently;
- use strategies appropriate to the needs of particular pupils;
- communicate informally with parents;
- complete ongoing assessments;

- attend and provide reports at review meetings;
- repeat the teacher's instructions to pupils when needed;
- read worksheets, ask the child to read the worksheet;
- ensure the pupil completes the work set and stays on task;
- provide opportunities for discussing their work;
- answer questions;
- ask questions to check understanding;
- accompany the child to the library to choose books;
- ensure pupils tidy up after sessions;
- use praise and encouragement to raise self-esteem;
- attend relevant training courses to raise awareness of support strategies and resources and feed this information back to the class teacher.

Case study

Alex James, a Year-6 teacher, wants a group of pupils who have been identified with learning difficulties and placed at School Action to produce a piece of independent work in history. The subject, 'A day in the life of a soldier in the Second World War', would be too much for this group without spelling support. They have limited skills when it comes to using the dictionary, so he asks his TA to produce some appropriate resources before the lesson:

Adrian, please prepare a bank of words, before the lesson, from this list for the red group for history. These are the words they are likely to need. Use the word bank sheet and type in these words and photocopy one for each child. I would like you to sit with yellow group, but please keep your eye on the red group too. Please keep a low profile as I want to see what they can do on their own. The word bank should help.

How we can help: supporting supply teachers

Supply teachers, who are often complete strangers to the school, may be uncertain about the role of the TA, and this may cause problems. The list in the handbook could be shown to the supply teacher at the beginning of a lesson to help them decide which of the tasks they would like TAs to perform. This clarifies the situation and provides understanding between the supply teacher and the TA, so that everyone is clear about who does what.

How we can help: supporting supply teachers

We can:
- take the register;
- supply a seating plan;
- indicate pupils with behaviour difficulties or special educational needs and show where the IEPs are kept;
- act as a behaviour monitor, recording the names of pupils who misbehave in order to report them to the teacher/headteacher;
- allow pupils a second chance if their behaviour improves, removing their name from the list;
- remind the supply teacher what the rules and sanctions are;
- explain what we normally do to support the class;
- act as a second pair of eyes by walking round the class;
- sit near to potential trouble-makers;
- remove very badly behaved pupils from the class;
- show where resources are kept;
- help line pupils up outside the classroom to ensure a settled entry;
- make sure that pupils sit in their correct places;
- show the supply teacher the list from this handbook entitled, *How we can help: in the classroom.*

Case study

Barbara Sharma is a supply teacher, and this is her first visit to the school. She has a TA, Liz, to support her in the morning and was very pleased that Liz gave her the lists entitled *How we can help: managing behaviour* and *How we can help: in the classroom.*

It was great to see the lists. It made things much clearer for me. It was such a good idea for her to take the register — I was able to take note of all the pupils and check their names against the seating plan Liz had given me. I have never really been sure before about what I can expect from the TA. I feel much more confident.

Additional ways in which we can support the school

This lists all the ways in which TAs are supporting the school in addition to the general classroom assistance.

Additional ways in which we can support the school

We also:
- run lunchtime clubs;
- sell tuck at breaktimes;
- organise the library;
- help to develop pupils' social skills by arranging and accompanying selected children at a special table (daily) in the school canteen, where pupils will:
  - eat their meals at a table set correctly with knife, fork, spoon and table napkin;
  - serve and be served food at the table from individual dishes;
  - talk with each other during the meal;
- organise breakfast clubs;
- help to keep the classroom safe and tidy;
- organise and display work on walls;
- collect appropriate artifacts for display areas;
- accompany teachers on school trips;
- support teachers in swimming lessons;
- assist at school productions and concerts;
- assist with the organisation of sports days, special assemblies etc.;
- organise after-school clubs for sewing, dance, drama and ICT;
- support pupils after school at a homework club;
- photocopy materials;
- collect money for school trips etc.;
- participate in out-of-school activities, e.g. the school summer fete.

Case study

Nadia Dambaza, the Year-2 teacher, noticed that some of the pupils in her class seemed very hungry in the mornings. Their mums said they would not eat breakfast at home. Nadia had read in a recent report that pupils' learning is affected if breakfast is not eaten. It is the most important meal of the day.

It would be great if some of our teaching assistants could establish a breakfast club before school. I know a lot of children do not have breakfast before they arrive and I know they will be much more likely to eat it if they are with their friends. Could it be organised?

References

Birkett, Veronica (2003) *How to Support and Teach Pupils with Special Educational Needs*, Wisbech: LDA

Department for Education and Employment (1998) *National Literacy Strategy: A Framework for Teaching Literacy*, London: DfEE

Department for Education and Employment (1999) *The National Numeracy Strategy: Framework for Teaching Mathematics*, London: DfEE

Department for Education and Skills (2000) *Teaching Assistants File – Induction for Teaching Assistants*, Nottingham: DfES

Department for Education and Skills (2000) *Working with Teaching Assistants: A Good Practice Guide*, London: DfES

Lee, Barbara (2002) *Teaching Assistants in Schools: The Current State of Play*, NFER

Lee, Barbara and Mawson, Clare (1998) *Survey of Classroom Assistants*, NFER

Local Government National Training Organisation (2001) *National Occupational Standards for Teaching/Classroom Assistants*, London: LGNTO
www.lg-employers.gov.uk/skills/teaching/download.html

Morris, Elizabeth (2002) *Insight Primary: Assessing and Developing Self Esteem*, NFER Nelson

Office for Standards in Education (2002) *Teaching Assistants in Primary Schools. An Evaluation of the Quality and Impact of their Work*, HMI Report 434

Primary Education: Raising Standards (1959) Her Majesty's Stationery Office

Raising Standards and Tackling Workloads: A National Agreement
www.teachernet.gov.uk/remodelling

Smith, Alistair (1996) *Accelerated Learning in the Classroom*, Network Educational Press

Further reading for teachers and teaching assistants

Balshaw, Maggie (2000) *Help in the Classroom*, London: David Fulton

Balshaw, Maggie and Farrell, Peter (2002) *Teaching Assistants. Practical Strategies for Effective Classroom Support*, London: David Fulton

Birkett, Veronica (2002) *How to Survive and Succeed as a Teaching Assistant*, Wisbech: LDA

Department for Education and Skills (2000) *Teaching Assistants File – Induction for Teaching Assistants*, Nottingham: DfES

Fox, Glenys (1998) *A Handbook for Learning Support Assistants: Teachers and Assistants Working Together*, London: David Fulton

Fox, Glenys (2001) *Supporting Children with Behaviour Difficulties: A Guide for Assistants in Schools*, London: David Fulton

Fox, Glenys and Halliwell, Marian (2000) *Supporting Literacy and Numeracy: A Guide for Learning Support Assistants*, London: David Fulton

Grant, Kate (2000) *Supporting Literacy: A Guide for Primary Classroom Assistants*, London: Routledge Falmer

Kay, Janet (2002) *Teaching Assistant's Handbook*, London: Continuum

Mackinnon, Cecilie (2003) *Teaching Strategies and Resources: A Practical Guide for Primary Teachers and Classroom Assistants*, London: David Fulton

Watkinson, Anne (2003) *The Essential Guide for Competent Teaching Assistants: Meeting National Occupational Standards at Level 2*, London: David Fulton

Watkinson, Anne (2003) *The Essential Guide for Experienced Teaching Assistants: Meeting the National Occupational Standards at Level 3*, London: David Fulton

Watkinson, Anne (2003) *Managing Teaching Assistants: Assisting Teaching and Learning*, London: Routledge Falmer